Y0-BVF-256

4.26.78

HOSTAGE

Murray S. Miron
Arnold P. Goldstein
Syracuse University

Behaviordelia, Inc.
Kalamazoo, Michigan

Library of Congress Cataloging in Publication Data
Miron, Murray S.
  Hostage

  Bibliography: p.
  1. Abduction.   2. Hostages—Case studies.   3. Law
enforcement. I. Goldstein, Arnold P., joint author. II. Title.
HV6571.M57   364.1'54'0926   77-16554
ISBN 0-914-47432-4

© 1978 Behaviordelia, Inc.
PO Box 1044
Kalamazoo, Michigan 49005

1   2   3   4   5   6   7   8   9
5   4   3   2   1   0   9   8   7

Printed and bound in U.S.A.

Cover design: Michael Frazier

To all those who do
and even those who may
only try to teach

Contents

The Authors

Murray S. Miron (PhD, University of Illinois) is Professor and Division Director of Psycholinguistics at Syracuse University, where he also directs the Honors program in psychology. He has pioneered work in the area of the analysis of threats, and in that capacity has served or is serving as a consultant to, among others, the Federal Bureau of Investigation, the Treasury Department, the State Department, the US Army and the Royal Canadian Mounted Police. He has also helped to develop the hostage-training program for the New York State Police and has been involved in a number of crisis incidents from Alaska to Florida. Some of his most publicized cases have included the search for the "Son of Sam" killer and the Hearst kidnappers. Dr. Miron is the only civilian to have received the Golden Badge Award for outstanding service (granted by the Central New York Chapter of the International Association of Chief's of Police). In addition to many books and articles, he has written *Reaction to Threat; Psycholinguistic Analyses of Coercion; Psycholinguistic Analyses of the Symbionese Liberation Army; Aural Coding in Language Processing;* and edited *Readings in the Psychology of Language,* and *Approaches to the Study of Aphasia*.

Arnold P. Goldstein (PhD. The Pennsylvania State University) brings to this book his expertise in *Structured Learning Therapy* and skill training in numerous facets of police crisis intervention. His recent book on that subject *(Police Crisis Intervention: A Structured Learning Manual)* has been widely adopted by colleges, and is being used by police departments as a training manual. A professor of psychology at Syracuse University, Dr. Goldstein's main areas of interest include behavior modification, skill training, interpersonal relationships, and aggression and control. Among the books he was written, co-authored or edited are *Helping People Change; Psychotherapy and the Psychology of Behavior Change; The Lonely Teacher; The Investigation of Psychotherapy; Structured Learning Therapy; Skill Training for Community Living;* and *Changing Supervisor Behavior*.

Preface

As the frequency and complexity of hostage situations has grown rapidly in the United States and around the world, it has become more and more important that we understand such situations more fully, and increase our ability to resolve them effectively. These two goals, better understanding and more skilled handling, are the dual purposes of this book. Regarding the perpetrators in hostage situations, we seek to provide information to better understand who they are, what motivates them and, most important, by what means we are likely to be successful in changing their behavior. What type of individual is best selected to serve as negotiator, how is he to be selected, and what are the specific negotiation procedures he best use to safely and effectively resolve the hostage situation? We seek to provide at least partial answers to these questions, as well as a detailed presentation of a training method for rapidly and successfully teaching law enforcement personnel the procedures necessary to function as effective negotiators.

The chapters which follow draw upon our own experience as consultants to law enforcement agencies in hostage and other crisis situations, the experience of valued colleagues in these arenas, and the fund of knowledge in the psychology of personality and persuasion so relevant to the topic of this book. Chapter one is an introduction to hostage negotiation and provides a number of the major themes of information we wish to share. Chapters two through five are case studies of actual hostage situations. They reflect these informational themes, provide a variety of hostage illustrations, and are examples of the many specific procedures involved in successful hostage negotiation.

The role of the media in hostage situations continues to represent a source of conflicting viewpoints. In chapter six we discuss some of the inherent problems with and procedures for dealing with media's place in hostage negotiation. In chapter seven we move to the specific procedures for negotiation and systematically spell them out. This chapter has been designed for the interested reader to use as part of his specific curriculum in negotiator training. While chapter seven provides the reader with **what** should be taught in negotiator training, chapters eight and nine seek to provide **how** to teach it. They are chapters concretely describing *Structured Learning Training*, a teaching method used effectively in the past to train police trainees in hostage management and crisis intervention skills.

While the first five of these chapters were written by Miron, chapter six jointly, and the last three by Goldstein, we view this book as a truly collaborative effort. If using it helps "turn around" but a single hostage situation and lead it toward a successful outcome, our efforts will have been worthwhile.

1 / Introduction

Over the last decade, we have observed an awesome increase in certain forms of crime which have required that we develop new forms of law enforcement skills and techniques. The siege of hostage incidents, skyjackings and acts of terrorism have challenged us to respond with effective countermeasures which can control such crime — crimes which more often than not are as senseless and illogical in appearance as they are dangerous and destructive. The perpetrators of these crimes have demanded everything from the feeding of all of the poor and the freeing of all political prisoners, to having all whites get off the planet. No community is immune from this rampant disease.

At 3:07 P.M. on December 30, 1974, the winter afternoon of peaceful Olean, New York rang out to the sound of a fusilade of shots fired by a seventeen-year-old boy. Before that day was to end, three lay dead and eleven others lay wounded at the hands of a boy who most considered to be the pride of the town. From Chowchilla through Syracuse, Plattsburg to Dallas, incident after incident has festooned our newspapers. Who commits such crimes? What do we know about these perpetrators, their motives and their personalities? These are questions of psychology, psychology translated into the effective, practical, law enforcement control of such crimes. We do have answers, perhaps not all there is to know, but beginning answers which have been used, and which have worked. The kind of psychology we will want to concern ourselves with must be capable of producing specific strategical and tactical law enforcement responses which protect ourselves, the lives of the victims and end in the apprehension of the perpetrator.

The kind of psychology we need can do a number of very important things. It interprets the behavior of the criminal so that behavior becomes predictable, reducing our uncertainty in dealing with what otherwise would appear to be senseless, and thereby increasing our confidence in the effects of the strategies and tactics those interpretations provided. Without an understanding of the behavior of a criminal, when we are at a loss as to how to predict what he will do and how to most effectively respond to what he is doing, we cannot devise plans, we lose confidence in our decisions, and let our uncertainties give the perpetrator control of a situation which we must control. In the search for an understanding of hostage-barricade crimes, we first need to chart their anatomy — to divide the overall situation into its parts so that we can look at the influences of each. In this spirit, we now wish to examine a number of the major components involved in the typical hostage situation.

BACKGROUND

There is a background for every act — the set of circumstances and conditions which led up to the act. Knowledge of what these background circumstances may have been can obviously aid us in understanding the behavior observed by us at the moment of the crime. Such background information should include rap sheets, psychiatric information, family and personal history whenever available. But perhaps less obvious, we also need to know what general factors may have led up to the perpetrator's action. In instance after instance, perpetrators have been shown to be aware of the outcomes of previous crisis incidents and are stimulated to copy what they have seen. The profile of the skyjacker developed by the FAA indicated that nearly all of these men had a clipping file of the news stories about previous incidents. Their plans were based upon this background they had gathered. We, too, need to know that background.

Prior to the Olean incident in which Anthony Barbaro barricaded himself in his high school building, the seventeen-year-old Barbaro kept a notebook of his murderous plans. In some 40 pages, written over a period of months, Barbaro recorded details of the weapons he intended to use, his motivations and his intent to kill. Three months prior to his killings, Barbaro wrote the following entries in his journal:*

October 1, 1974
I get nothing but setbacks. I want to sleep for a long time. I haven't

---

*These entries were copied verbatim from the Barbaro journal.

quite decided if I'm going to die or not. I may walk out just to observe the reactions of others. The possibility of torturing the hostages has also entered my mind.
October 9, 1974
It's been awhile. Some new thoughts. What affect would a new Jack the Ripper have on this "fair community"?
October 10, 1974
This new alternative has become a powerful enticement. I've already seen some places for the murders. I could start on the last day of this month and repeat the Ripper's pattern exactly.
October 13, 1974
I've finished the book. The prime Ripper suspect sounded a lot like me; intelligent, but unstable. Pushed toward the edge of life's futility. I have serious thoughts on reproducing the Ripper's actions. I, however, have to be much better "prepared" than he; considering today's technology.
October 14, 1974
I've reconsidered recreating the Ripper murders. Due to the fact that today's police methods are far superior to those of 1888; that individual forces would work together rather than against each other as they did in 1888. All these facts have convinced me that such an action could jeopardize my major plan for assault against the futility called life.
The last entry in his journal reads:
My depression has reached an all-time low and I don't know why. It's now or never. I have to act or die; and I will not die!
I now have a total of four fully charged propane tanks. I'm hopeful their explosions will have a devastating effect. More good news. The rifle part I've been waiting so long for is now available. Soon I'll be ready to make my move. A prevalent symptom of my anxiety, paranoia, has reappeared. This, along with the depression I mentioned before also brings my angry hostility. For now, however, I'm still able to control it. It's amazing how a simple, insignificant thing like a Bill's (football game) loss can bring my killer depression. My home situation doesn't help matters. The sooner I can make my hit, the better. If I'm delayed for any reason, for any length of time, anything could happen.
Due to a recent psychology assignment, I've been able to discover some other's opinions of me. In a few words I'm nice, but withdrawn. They want me to open up, express myself, quite a funny notion, ironic! If someone had helped me do just that a couple of years ago, I probably would've turned out OK. But the

paranoia forced on me has made my withdrawal all but irrevers-
ible. My only release now is the attack.

Had personality information such as this, or even a sampling of it, been
available to law enforcement personnel at this barricade scene, certainly effective use could have been made of it.

Information which can be obtained about the personal background
of the perpetrator may tell us of special skills or knowledge which may
be critical in evaluating the credibility of his threats. In the Kiritsis
incident in Indianapolis (see Chapter three) it was critical that it be
known whether or not the apartment was rigged with high explosives
triggered to go off if a forced entry was attempted. Kiritsis' background
as a weapons instructor gave him the specialized skills that made his
threat credible, even though it turned out that he, in fact, had no high
explosives. Such background information might have to include intelligence information on groups or even such things as religious and
spiritual information as contained in the *Koran*, the holy book of the
Moslems. In Washington, such information provided the key to the
solution of the Hanafi Muslim siege. Knowing that the perpetrator is on
drugs or even that he smokes may provide the lever needed for
successful negotiation. In the Syracuse incident, where Leroy Cotton
was holding a pregnant girl and her 18-month-old baby, the negotiator, Lt. Galvin, was able to successfully bargain for the release of the
baby in trade for a few cigarettes, and eventually for Cotton's surrender for just one more cigarette.

At the scene of a crisis, negotiators will often be surrounded by
priests, relatives, friends and the merely curious who will be babbling
everything from, "He's a good boy," to "I knew he was crazy ever since
he took after me with that knife." Much of this is either irrelevant or
mistaken or both. What is needed is an organized checklist of the kinds
of information which are important in dealing with the perpetrator.
You need to know such things as:

Names: close relatives, children, girlfriends.

Criminal Record: how many arrests, and for what?

Psychiatric Record: has he been committed; has he been seeing a
psychiatrist; what's the psychiatrist's name; is he available?

Specialized Skills: what does he know about weapons, explosives,
etc.; can he fly, drive?

Special Affiliations: is he a member of a special group, religious
order, sect or gang; is he married; does he have children?

Deviations or Addictions: does he have any unusual habits; is he
homosexual; does he drink, gamble?

Immediate Problems: is he broke, jilted, hungry, drunk, high, being sued, paroled?*
All of these things can be important. Someone should be assigned to gather such background information, condense it, summarize it, pass it along and be ready to get more as the need may arise. Often, however, such information is slow in coming, can't be found and may be wrong. If we spend too much time gathering or waiting for background information, the situation may get ahead of us. We often need to use whatever background information can be obtained **rapidly**, as we put our first priority on the situation itself and what is given to us by the immediate behavior of the perpetrator. What he has done in the last 30 seconds may well be a better predictor of what he will likely do in the next 30 seconds than what he may have done 10 years ago.

SITUATION

Situations vary immensely. You have got to anticipate the unexpected, be ready to be flexible and avoid pat solutions. You must be able to tolerate enough ambiguity long enough to get law and order established. That may mean using whatever is at hand in the immediate situation. If you can think of 20 ways to use a brick for something other than building outhouses, you'll probably make a good negotiator. At the time of the initial response to a crisis, the situation is nearly always chaotic, emotions are high and the perpetrator is in control. We need to move the situation toward stability, calmness and containment. We need to tie up the loose ends, define the terms of the standoff and gradually impose our control. Containment must include the perpetrator, the spectators and the media. As in any crisis or disaster we need to establish a sterile perimeter free of bystanders and the curious. The thought uppermost should be that the crisis is a law enforcement operation.

During the emergency, no one else has any business at the scene, and that includes the well-meaning, the press, the "experts" and everyone else. If such are needed their presence should only be at the request of the officers in charge, and they should be informed that their permission can be revoked at any time. Fundamental as this may sound, it seems to us that we have on occasion forgotten this basic tenet of law enforcement, particularly with respect to the media. We need to have enough conviction to tell some reporters that they will be

---

*For a complete checklist indicating desirable background information to be obtained about the perpetrator, as well as his hostages, see Chapter 8, Section II.

subject to arrest if their activities are judged to be endangering the safety of you and the public, as they clearly on occasion have. When the media telephones the hostage-taker for an on-the-spot interview while you're trying to negotiate with him, or shows the location of your S.W.A.T. team in their televised coverage, they have clearly endangered the lives of others.

Everything that takes place at the scene of the crisis becomes part of the situation. Control of these extraneous influences extends to the law enforcement presence as well. A crisis should not have more response than is required to contain the situation. One hundred men armed with riot guns under loose fire-at-opportunity orders stand to shoot at least 10 of each other. We need to establish orderliness, authority and calm, all of which will readily occur if sufficient prior planning, coordination and training of personnel have been accomplished.

Orderliness, authority and calm translate into specific tactics, which mean that we should **not** have crowds, media, our own men, sirens, lights and other emergency measures visible to the perpetrator. Officers should take their positions unobtrusively, orders should be given sparingly and quietly, bull horns should be avoided. We want to establish the appearance of routineness — the ordinariness of the trained professional who has seen and dealt with numerous similar situations. We can't literally ignore the perpetrator much as that might be effective, but we can and should deny him the excitement he thinks his act may invoke. If we can calm the situation sufficiently to bring it to a standoff, and then continue to squeeze that situation down to the kind of box that has only one way out — our way — we will have accomplished what we want. There are just too many possibilities in a chaotic situation for us to begin to control them. We must from the outset move to establish order and to restrict the number of possibilities so that they are weighted in our favor. This also implies that we do not want to take actions which may only serve to complicate the situation.

Although the place where some hostage-taker may be holed up, for example, may present tactical problems, it is better to live with those problems than to attempt to move the perpetrator to some location more to our liking. Bringing relatives or others to the perpetrator, taking him to them, exchanging hostages, too readily making concessions all act to increase the complication of the situation and should be avoided. Some of these actions, as we shall see, can produce the sort of complications which can be lethal. In one incident, the police escorted an armed man who had been threatening suicide to the apartment of the girlfriend who had jilted him. When they reached the building, they found that the door to the apartment house was locked and had to wait until they could get it open. When they finally reached the apartment door of the girlfriend and asked that she try to convince him not to go through with his suicide, the new lover of the girl shouted through the closed door that she was not going to talk to anybody. At that point, the victim killed himself.

Let me hasten to point out, lest I (author Miron) leave the wrong impression, that when we speak of narrowing down the options open to a perpetrator, we must bear in mind that we don't want **him** to see it that way. From his standpoint we want him to believe that our solution to this problem is best for him. It is even better if we can prod him into thinking that he not only thought up the solution but had to convince us to comply. Most of these kinds of perpetrators are losers who have lived lives of failure. They are inept in nearly everything they have tried. They are lousy problem-solvers who most of the time only seem to think that bricks are for breaking windows. But they are human and like everybody else they have not accepted the world's judgment that they are failures. They need to feel, and typically do delude themselves into feeling, that they are smart, significant and successful, or at least blame the failures they can't deny on you, the world, their backgrounds or anything else even remotely handy.

The Time Factor

If there is one generalization that has come from experience in these sorts of situations, it is that time is our best ally. If we can move past the early minutes of a crisis and bring some sort of stability to the situation, the longer it remains stable, the higher the probability that it will end favorably. This has even been true for those situations in which one or more hostages have been initially killed. There are a number of reasons why time is on our side. First, it acts to calm the situation. In a crisis the body quickly mobilizes adrenalin which surges through the blood stream, converts stored glycogen into sugar, redistributes blood to the extremities, increases heart output, causes sweating, dilation of the pupils and a general, diffuse energization of the body. These responses use up body energy at a greatly accelerated rate and cannot be sustained for long periods. Over time, the body begins to respond with a rebound effect of insulin discharge which destroys the sugar and leaves the individual feeling worn out, sluggish and depressed. It is this later phase that we need, and time alone will produce it.

Incidentally, it should be pointed out that the same effects work on us. In those incidents which extend over a long period of time you need to fight the depression which will begin to take hold of you. In the Syracuse incident, it was vital that the negotiator be given food and coffee. Part of my (author Miron) job in assisting the police negotiator during that 13-hour siege was to make sure that Lt. Galvin had sugar in his coffee. Time also serves to produce one of the weirdest phenomenon we have seen in such crises — the so-called **Stockholm-Effect** — named after a hostage incident in Sweden in which one of the female hostages fell in love with and married one of the perpetrators. The effect, although seemingly incredible does occur and should be expected. Actually, the phenomenon has been known for quite some time. Psychologists have alternatively called it either introjection or identification with the aggressor.

By any name, the effect works in our favor. As time progresses, the victim and perpetrator begin to develop a rapport in which each begins to change his attitudes towards those of the other. From the standpoint of the victim, this change in feelings has high survival value. From our standpoint, the change can produce some complications we should be aware of. As the effect takes hold, it will often be the case that the victim begins to work in concert with the perpetrator and against us. If given a chance to escape, for example, the victim may choose to remain with his captor, argue for concessions for the perpetrator and generally try to protect his tormentor. In incident after incident we have seen examples of such behavior which can only be described as bizarre. Because I am certain that many readers will remain justifiably skeptical, let me give you a few actual examples.

In February of 1970, during the diversion of an Eastern Airlines flight from Miami to Cuba, the skyjacker at one point handed his .45 caliber pistol to the flight engineer to hold for him while he accepted a drink from the stewardess. After the abductor finished his drink, the first engineer handed the weapon back to him. Interviewed after the event, this crew member, although fully aware that at that point in the skyjacking the criminal had been completely disarmed, stated that the skyjacker was really a nice guy and that he didn't want to be the one responsible for having his attempt fail.

The Hearst kidnapping probably represents one of the most dramatic instances of the effect. After being kidnapped and held in a closet for some period of time, Patty Hearst actually joined the SLA as one of their devoted members. Defreeze, the self-styled field marshal of that organization, is said to have actually wanted her to leave his group because he was skeptical about her conversion to their cause.

Nonetheless, the general public reaction was that Patty must have been a part of the plan from the outset. They could not believe that any such effect could be possible.

The effect works both ways. Not only does the victim begin to identify with his captor, but the captor with the victim as well. It is this form of identification which makes it difficult for the hostage-taker to harm his victims. In general, the longer we can keep the perpetrator and his victims together in a situation which gives them a chance to interact with one another, the safer the hostage will be. In a number of instances in which the victims were hooded, the hostages have been killed, possibly because the hooding acted to prevent the development of any relationship between them and the perpetrator. We, too, can destroy the opportunity for such interaction if we continually force the perpetrator to respond to us rather than to his victims. Thus, it is generally sound tactical procedure to give the hostage-taker opportunities to get to know his victims.

Other Tactics

Tactics such as turning off the power should generally be avoided. However, if the media is broadcasting information which should be kept from the perpetrator, it is better to risk the suspicion the blackout will create. Turning off the heat **is** an effective tactic for producing the sort of deprivation conditions which will help to convince the perpetrator that he is better off giving up. As noted earlier, it is also recommended that a show of massed force be avoided. This advice does not apply in those situations where an immediate mobilization of force or an assault can be expected to be successful. Prison riots or mob actions are generally best handled by an immediate show of force. The difference in such situations is that the perpetrators should not be permitted to establish rapport with one another. At the outset such loosely banded groups have divergent interests and concerns. But the longer they are allowed to interact and the more you seem to concede to them, the stronger the bonds of mutually shared goals will become. If you can break the group apart into individuals at the outset, you have focused on the mob's weakness. Exactly the opposite may be true for terrorist groups who have self-selected their membership and have interacted together over a long period of time. Any attempt to break such groups into individual components may result in failure if the members are more afraid of the consequences of treason to the group than they are of you, or even of death.

THE PERPETRATOR

These last points regarding the situation also obviously relate to questions regarding the psychology of the perpetrator. It will be useful for us to discuss different types of perpetrators in terms of the meaning of their behavior. In particular, we wish to divide perpetrators into two major classifications: those engaging in **instrumental** behavior and those enacting **expressive** behavior. By an instrumental act, we will mean any action on the part of a perpetrator which has some recognizable goal which the perpetrator seeks to have fulfilled and which will constructively benefit him. A fleeing felon acts instrumentally when he attempts to bargain for his escape. The extortionist seeks instrumental personal gain at the expense of someone else. By expressive acts we will mean all those acts which serve only to display the power or significance of the perpetrator – acts which appear to be senseless in that there is no obvious way in which the perpetrator can stand to gain anything or in which the act is clearly self-destructive. The Olean sniping incident was such an act.

Frequently, an act may begin as instrumental and end being expressive, or the act can be both at once. In such instances, it is important for us to sort out and deal with each of the components with strategies which are appropriate to each. Let's consider suicide situations. A suicide threat can be either instrumental or expressive. If the potential suicider seeks to have someone else comply with his demands at the threat of his killing himself, he is behaving instrumentally. The jilted girlfriend who threatens to kill herself if you don't take her back clearly wishes to coerce you into giving her what she wants. Her attempt is to play upon your guilt by attempting to make you responsible for her death. The situation is entirely analogous to that of a mugger who enforces his demands with a gun.

Suicides can also be expressive acts. The death of the victim is a statement of despair and rejection shouted to the world. As expression, it is the desperation of those who believe they cannot be heard in any other way. In general, for either form of act, the fact that the individual has given us a chance to respond to his threat, itself indicates that negotiation in the one case and listening in the other can avert the suicide. There are instances, however, in which the instrumental or expressive utility of a suicide is so powerful that the individual will carry through his threat no matter what we do.

Here are some general guidelines, which should be tried in any attempted suicide. Avoid discussions with the potential suicider which focus on intellectual or abstract moral principles. Death in the abstract is tidy and clean. The evidence we have collected is that suiciders who succeeded in their attempts have been those who intellectualized their experiences. Concentrate instead on the immediate, the senses and the ordinary: You're hungry, aren't you? It's stuffy in here, isn't it? Do you want to share a cigarette with me? These are the sorts of questions which are difficult to philosophize about. Avoid conveying an attitude of solemness or high drama, both of which only increase the tension. Don't bring more spectators or loved ones to the scene, they provide the audience the suicider may wish to express himself before.

From what I (author Miron) have said, it should be clear that in my opinion clergymen and priests head the list of "don'ts" if they intend to discuss philosophy with the suicider. Give the victim a chance to back down without losing face. Remember that he has announced to the world that he is going to commit a drastic act; if he doesn't, he will have to face himself and that world tomorrow. We recommend that the threatener be arrested and led out in handcuffs. This is delicate. You shouldn't, of course, threaten arrest, but you can make clear by implication that your presence as a law enforcement officer implies that he will have to come with you. The point is that the world can plainly see when you emerge together that **you** prevented him from taking his life, that he wanted to do it and was prepared to do it, but **you** stopped him. At the very least, never agree to leave him alone if he promises to come out after you have gone. He comes with you or you don't leave.

Many acts of terrorism are really acts of expressive suicide. They have as their sole purpose the establishment of the significance and importance of the perpetrator. They are acts designed to establish the perpetrator's importance through media coverage. Often the perpetrators mask these true intentions through the facade of some worthy, or at least respectable, cause. Thus, what appears to be instrumental behavior is only expresssive. It is in this sense that we can say that every human action typically has a number of different purposes. Sorting through these multiple purposes of any given act is difficult but vital. Otherwise you may find yourself responding to the obvious or manifest content of an act and only making the hidden or latent problem worse. Here is where psychological expertise can be of immense aid. Properly used, such expertise can be employed to read the latent content of the perpetrator's behavior and suggest tactics which will address these hidden problems. Let's use the example of the SLA again to illustrate this point.

Defreeze and his cohorts took Patricia Hearst hostage as an action of the people's forces in order to have the poor of California fed. When it was pointed out to them that their demands would require literally billions of dollars, they became progressively more confused, until it became clear that their intent was really to punish the world at large for the personal oppression they felt they had suffered at its hands. In order to gain sympathy for themselves they needed to paint themselves as innocents who had been and continued to be unjustly persecuted by the violence of the law and the "rip-off" of the capitalists. The attempt to apprehend them was, in their view, evidence of our violence. We were the guilty, they were the innocents.

Such reverse logic is characteristic of the paranoid personality. It projects the blame for its own anger and resentment onto others around it. The oppression with which the SLA was concerned was really the oppression of their own guilt. The punishment they sought to visit upon the world was the product of their own resentment. Under such conditions it was entirely predictable that they would engineer the final showdown so that lethal force would be required. I am convinced that Defreeze and his followers in that house in Los Angeles died believing they were innocent and proud to have proven how violent **we** were. In fact, those were the exact terms that the surviving Harrises used in eulogizing their dead comrades.

To further understand the nature of the perpetrator in such situations, let's look in some detail at still another example of a dramatic hostage-taking incident. A light drizzle had been falling over most of the southern seaboard since five on the morning of February 22, 1974. At Baltimore-Washington International, Delta Flight 523 bound for Atlanta and Columbus was being readied for an 0715 departure. Forty-nine passengers and Samuel J. Byck planned to board the flight, but Byck's plans were different from any of the other travelers of that morning. While Captain Reese Loftin and First Officer Fred Jones were making their preflight weather and routing checks, Samuel Byck was sitting in his car tape-recording his justifications for his plan to commandeer Flight 523. This recording, made by a man who was to murder two people and finally commit suicide, represents one of the most significant criminal documents in the search for an understanding of the nature of pathological perpetrator behavior. In less than 10 minutes of monologue, he provides an invaluable glimpse into the mind of one who could plan and execute such a seemingly senseless crime.

Byck's act must be viewed within the context of the background of what had been happening before his crime. February 22, 1974 had marked 13 months in which the United States had successfully deterred skyjacking attempts. The infamous Southern Airlines skyjacking had occurred on January 2, 1973 and was the last of an epidemic wave of such incidents. But in 1974, the newspapers were crowded with reports of the kidnapping of the Atlanta Constitution editor, J. Reginald Murphy, and the negotiations with the abductors of Patricia Hearst. The New York Police Department had discovered several million dollars of heroin and cocaine missing from their property office, and a thousand muggings, assaults and routine criminalities festooned the back pages of papers across the nation.

Nor was this the first time the authorities had cause to be concerned with 44-year-old Samuel Byck. In 1972, Byck had written then President Nixon of his grievances and had threatened to take action. In 1973, he had been committed for psychiatric examination following two arrests by the Federal Park Police for picketing the White House without a permit. Released after these arrests on judicial determination that no permit was required for picketing by a single individual, Byck again picketed wearing a Santa Claus costume on Christmas Eve of 1973. Interviewed by the press at that time, Byck asserted that "All I want for Christmas is my constitutional right to publicly petition my government for a redress of grievances. I want to see if they have the guts to arrest Santa Claus." Before his skyjacking attempt Byck said:

> The Chinese have a toast that they drink and it goes: "May you live in interesting times, may you live in interesting times." This should be a little interesting anyhow, oughta make some sort of conversation. There's also a little side by-play here also, for I don't think there has been a successful skyjacking in a little over a year. That should be interesting to see how that one works out. Interesting times, interesting times.

At approximately 0700 hours, Byck entered the sterile corridor leading to the loading area for Delta Flight 523. George Ramsburg, the airport security guard, was stationed at the magnetometer. Approaching him from behind, Byck fired his .22 caliber pistol directly into the guard's head, killing him almost instantly. Byck then boarded the plane carrying an incendiary device consisting of two gallons of gasoline wired to an ignition mechanism in an attaché case. Eight passengers had already boarded the plane when Byck burst into the flight cabin brandishing his gun. After securing the forward entrance door, he commanded the pilot to "fly this plane out of here." When the crew failed to comply, explaining that the wheels were still chocked, Byck went to the passenger compartment to secure a woman as hostage and then shot and wounded both the pilot and first officer.

Outside the plane, Police Officer Charles Troyer had unsuccessfully tried to shoot out the tires of the aircraft with his .38 service revolver. Returning to the body of his dead colleague, Troyer removed Ramsburg's .357 magnum and succeeded in deflating the tires. During this time Byck had returned his first hostage to the passenger cabin and taken a second female hostage to the cockpit where he again had shot Captain Loftin and Copilot Jones, killing Jones and critically wounding Loftin. Troyer then fired through the aircraft windows and scored two hits in Byck's chest and abdomen. Either would have been sufficient to have eventually caused Byck's death, but Byck's immediately following shot through his own temple was determined by the coroner to have been the direct cause of his death.

Byck did not act out of sudden impulse. There is direct evidence that he had planned his crime for more than six months. What meaning can be given to an act which took the lives of three human beings? Who was Byck at the moment of his crime? In this instance we have Byck's own words to analyze for the answers. The traditional psychiatric approach to an understanding of Byck would have attempted to identify those incidents in his past which had brought him to BWI Airport on the last day of his life, but the law enforcement officer rarely has the luxury of such techniques. As often as not the criminal is an anonymous menace who must be dealt with on the instant. When such instantaneous response is necessary, it may not be helpful to know that Byck may have had an unhappy childhood and a dissatisfying marriage which had ended in divorce a year earlier. While such background information, when time is available, can be useful, the material which can be of maximum effectiveness in such cases is the behavior and communications of the perpetrator at the time of his crime. There is in these communications the coded material which can lead us to the responses which can be expected to maximize the effectiveness of our responses to the perpetrator. We shall use this technique on Byck's communication. He begins his account of himself in the tape recording made just prior to his entering the airport with the following declarations: "I should have been better prepared, but unfortunately I'm not. This tape seems to be spinning awfully fast. I wonder if I've done something wrong. According to my watch it's now twenty minutes to six. I have less than two hours."

Throughout the tape, Byck is preoccupied with time. The tape appears to be spinning "awfully fast." His watch tells him he has "less than two hours." And later he says: "In less than an hour I will be moving toward the airport." He mourns the lack of time he feels he needed to be "better prepared." We know that Byck had more than an appointment to catch a flight; he had an appointment with his own death. Byck is experiencing the time-distorting effects of what is technically known as the "dissociative reaction." This reaction is one in which an individual under extreme stress feels as if he is watching himself from somewhere outside his own body or in another part of his own mind. It is the common report of many who may perform acts of extreme heroism in the face of mortal danger. They indicate that it was as if they were watching themselves in an unreal, slow motion dream for which they disbelievingly only realize the danger to themselves after the act.

While Byck is in this condition, he is oblivious to danger or harm; he is incapable of perceiving or evaluating any personal risk to himself. The condition produces a paradoxical calmness as a direct response to the anxiety and stress which is the normal reaction to anticipated violence. Where we have a chance to react to the perpetrator, we need to impress upon him by our actions and words that we are in no hurry to meet any deadlines, that we have all the time in the world. The perpetrators will frequently ask what time it is and set various time deadlines for some action. Never respond with an exact time or appear to be panicked by his deadlines. Never remind the perpetrator of time. Every deadline that passes is another victory for us and makes the perpetrator more indecisive. Byck says:

> I don't feel too badly. I felt jittery before, you know, months ago or even weeks ago just thinking of it. Maybe it was true what Thoreau said when he said, "We have nothing to fear but fear." I don't know if I'm afraid, but I don't seem jittery at least right now, maybe later I will be . . . here I am, calm, cool, collected and tired.

Immediately after being troubled by the speed of his tape recorder, Byck's next thoughts concern his identification and position. He says:

> I've got all of my identification out of here . . I don't have any identification on me. I don't know if I should be parked here in the expensive parking lot, but since I'm not going to pay it doesn't make much difference. Maybe I should be parked in another place. It all depends on how soon they find the car. I'd like the car to stay hidden for a while.

The ludicrousness of Byck's concern over being in the premium parking lot becomes meaningful only when the communication is treated as code. His own rationalization for the self-evident absurdity of worrying about the higher parking rate in terms of finding his car is patently false. His real concern seems to be that he simply does not belong in a parking lot used by the important, prestigious people who travel by air. Following as an association to his identification, this concern regarding his proper place is to be interpreted as his perception of himself as unimportant and insignificant. It is this true identity which he wishes to remain hidden for as long as possible while he plays at the role of being the important, decisive, dangerous skyjacker. If the authorities knew what he knows to be true of himself, Byck is convinced that they would not take him seriously and could deter him from his assumed role.

Dr. Harvey Schlossberg, the psychologist in charge of the New York City Police Department Special Training Program for Crisis Management, has related the story of the bank robber who upon entering the bank and finding lines before the teller cages stood in the queue to commit his robbery because he didn't wish to take someone's place in line. Dr. David Hubbard has documented numerous incidences in his extensive studies of the skyjacker in which the crime could have been or was aborted by merely putting the perpetrator in his place. In one incident in Plattsburg, a thirty-year state police veteran merely went up to an armed hostage-taker who was holding three victims and demanded that he turn over his gun, and the perpetrator immediately complied.

Daily and Pickrel, the FAA staff psychologists responsible for the development of the skyjacker profile and the inflight defense programs, report that "the original studies of the psychological nature of hijackers led to the conclusion that as a group they are neither very resourceful nor very determined. They have not been the long-haired hippy types but more the "hanger-on," hustler types found around a bus depot late at night. They also seem to be a very different sort of social subgroup than that represented by the usual air traveler. The usual air traveler, such as the businessman, is a successful member of society, but hijackers, as a group, are its failures." This description could equally well serve for most of the hostage-takers society has recently seen.

On the one hand Byck is saying that he should be parked in the prestigious lot, but on the other hand should be parked in another place. Such an analysis immediately suggests methods which might have aborted Byck's crime. His conflicting indecisiveness might have been turned against him. If he could have been reminded of who he was, and that this act like all his others would fail, his own certainty of his failure might have tipped the conflict away from violence to capture. In terms of specific tactics this means that we should periodically ask the perpetrator during our negotiations to give up. It is amazing that in a number of instances, the hostage-taker has indicated after his arrest that he would have given up sooner, but that no one asked him to. Byck attempts his own explanation of what he is about to do. He says:

If there is a moral to this madness, I suspect it may be the expression, "am I my brother's keeper," and the answer would have to be positively yes. For we are all brothers and if any one of us is hurting then we all stand to get hurt. I've never owned a pistol or even fired a pistol. It's rather strange. I'm not possessed by guns. I think they're weapons to kill, and it was only when I realized that killing and being killed may have to be done before men begin to respect other men. I think this all begins with a lack of respect, so I've got the gun and the time is beginning to run out on me. They can call me misguided if they like, but of course, being misguided or being guided is only a matter again of who's interpreting the action and what side of the fence you're sitting on. I feel that I'm guided, that I have a purpose, and I think that I've made it abundantly clear what I think my purpose is. I have a motivation, and that's it.

Notice how similar these words are to those of Barbaro's just before the Olean incident. Both men needed to justify their acts, were concerned with how they would be viewed by others and seemed to be driven to violence despite themselves. Byck's life had been one of continuous failure. Born 44 years ago in Philadelphia, he had worked at many unsatisfying jobs in his lifetime. Unemployed at the time of the attempted skyjack, his last job had been as a salesman. He had been divorced a year before. His language was childlike in character. He had been hurt, so he intended to hurt back in a temper tantrum display of his resentment. He was no more insane than any small child who angrily throws his toys about because he has been denied some indulgence. As an adult and not a child, he was continually faced by the incongruity of his own high opinion of himself and his failures. Dismissed by most as a harmless crank, by his wife as ineffectual, and by the world as a loser, he intended to show them all that he was none of these things.

Hostage-taking crimes which are not obviously instrumental in character are often to be understood as instrumental attempts to punish and terrorize the onlooker. It is in this sense that the taking of a hostage is an act of terrorism. Its aim is to frighten and dominate the innocent observer of the incident. The wider the fear engendered, the more powerful and successful the offender. The actual hostages in such crimes have more often than not been afforded benevolent treatment by the offender. Notice that Byck actually had taken two of the women passengers as hostages and had shot the pilots rather than them. These women who were forced to witness the shootings may well have represented symbols of all of the women in his life whom he believed to have unjustly oppressed him. They, like those in the crowded airport outside who had been forced to watch the security guard being killed were being punished by Byck for his failures.

The more over-reactive our responses, the more **we** cower or lash back with fear or resentment, the greater the punishment the criminal visits upon us. The tactic required that the criminal behave in a manner which impresses his audience that he is innocent and more victim than aggressor, or at least that his actions are justified by what others have done to him. It is important for him to establish this image to his audience. Byck's entire tape recording is one long justification of his innocence. His rationalization for his act implies that any retaliation will be unjustified. He is the victim, not the aggressor. Even after being mortally wounded, he commits suicide.

In the Indianapolis incident, the authorities feared that Kiritsis might hear of the dozens of calls they had gotten from citizens who felt that the real estate agent he was holding deserved anything he got. As a society we applaud violence when that violence is made to appear justified. Some of you, reading this now, may be saying to yourself that these guys we are talking about should be killed. The criminals feed upon such over-reaction and use it to enlist sympathies from the audience against you. If we over-react, we encourage others to attempt to seek the sympathy of the audience such over-reaction will produce.

One is constantly struck by the inadequacy of the problem-solving capability of the hostage-taker. The range of potential solutions which such inadequate personalities perceive as available is remarkably small. Negotiation in hostage/barricade crises is simply the process of providing the criminal with a wider range of productive solutions to his problems. Byck exhibits a dramatic reduction of his problem-solving intellect. His act is to be understood as an act of suicide. His self-perceptions of worthlessness, helplessness and lack of significance lead him to the limiting conclusion that only "killing or being killed" will redress his grievances. Suicide is no less suicide if an individual's behavior compels another to his own murder. It is in this sense that we should attempt to avoid, if at all possible, solving a hostage situation through assault tactics. The violence may serve to only stimulate others to attempt to make us responsible for their deaths. Byck knew that his act of air piracy was punishable by death and that he would probably be killed in the attempt. Far from deterring him, it acted as an attraction to him much as a moth is attracted to the flame which consumes it. Byck says:

To Bonny, I drink a toast, although I left my Grand-dad at home. No booze, no drugs, no rah-rah-rah, no nothing. No flags flying of any color or description, just a job I feel has to be done for mankind. I feel not like a hero, not like a terrorist. I think that if I were to have a grave rather than to be, ah what do they call it when they burn you up, cremated. I think a tombstone that I would like to have is that: "He didn't like what he saw and he decided to do something about it." I just wish that I don't get to be known as a maniac or madman. There are a lot of things that I am, but those are two things that I'm not; a maniac or madman. It's always easy for the authorities to look outward for the causes to say this guy acted as a madman, a mad dog and this guy acted as a maniac when basically the causes of these hostile actions, or at least my hostile actions are inward; that of being robbed and cheated out of my dignity and seeing my country being raped and ravished almost before my very eyes and I won't stand idly by and allow it to happen.

As those who are charged with the task of somehow not letting happen the sorts of things Byck, Barbaro and all those like them have attempted, it is our job to both understand them and control them.

2 / The Cotton Case

Syracuse, New York is a city of moderate size situated some 300 miles north of New York City and 150 miles east of Buffalo. Syracuse had never had a major hostage incident until the morning of February 25, 1977. Between the Kiritsis incident in Indianapolis and the Hanafi Muslim incident in Washington, Syracuse suddenly was faced with a problem many thought could only happen in "those other places."

At approximately 0200 hours, Leroy Cotton, a 27-year-old black male shot and killed one George Sparks and then barricaded himself in a neighboring apartment, holding seven-month pregnant Earline Jones and her 18-month-old baby as hostages for more than 13 hours. This incident, in most regards, can be considered "typical" of such problems, and warrants detailed examination for the lessons it can provide.

Earline Jones

We shall begin by letting Earline Jones, the principal victim, relate in her own words the circumstances which led up to the incident. She says:*

On the night of February 24, 1977, Thursday evening, I had gotten home from my mother's house. I went next door to JoAnn Jones' apartment and JoAnn was telling me that her and Marvin Austin was arguing over leaving town. So I asked JoAnn to walk me to

---

*Changes have been made in Earline's statement where required in order to clarify her narrative and to correct spelling and punctuation. Otherwise, the statements which follow are exactly as they were written and given to the District Attorney.

the store and we went to the store. I got a pack of cigarettes and went home. JoAnn stayed at the house for about 10 minutes and then she left. Ten minutes later Marvin Austin came up and we was talking about him and JoAnn leaving Syracuse (to go) to Chicago. While Marvin was there, Tony Lee Thomas came upstairs and asked me if Leroy Cotton was home. I told him no. So he said there was something in Leroy's apartment he had to get that was very important. Tony said if we heard any noises to ignore them. So me and Marvin kept quiet.

The next thing I heard was Tony kicking (down) the door to Leroy Cotton's apartment. He managed to kick in the wood of the door and he unlocked it and went in. The next thing I knew was Tony was coming out and he said when Leroy came back to tell him he kicked the door open cause there was something inside he needed and (that) he (would) be right back. After Tony left, Marvin left and George Sparks came up. Me and George was sitting down talking. About 11:00 my sister (Bell Jones) came up and asked me what was I going to cook. I said, "Chicken." Then Leroy came up the stairs and asked what happened to his door. I told him that Tony kicked it in cause there was something he had to get and (Leroy) said he would wait for Tony to come back. I told Bell to ask Leroy if he had a sharp knife so that I could cut up some chicken. He said no, he only had a butter knife, so my sister Bell stayed in his apartment for half an hour.

In the meantime, I went over to JoAnn's apartment and asked her to let me hold her sharp knife so I could cook some chicken. JoAnn asked me who all was at my house and I told her my sister, George and the baby. She said she would be up in a little while and I said OK. I came back to my apartment and George and the baby was playing on the couch. As I was getting the chicken ready to fry, I needed black pepper, so I went next door and asked Leroy to let me borrow his pepper and he passed it through the door. As he passed it, I peeked in and all the lights were out except the bedroom light and Leroy was half dressed. So I took the pepper and went back in my apartment and fried the chicken. JoAnn came up and asked where was my sister and I told her she was in Leroy's apartment and she said what was she doing? I said, "I don't know." And JoAnn said, "How long she been in there ? And I said, "For a half hour." JoAnn left and me and George was teasing her by telling her that her boyfriend was coming. Ten minutes later, JoAnn came back. Then Bell came out of Leroy's apartment smiling and me, JoAnn and George was teasing Bell.

JoAnn and Bell started arguing 'cause Bell had been over there and didn't get no money. So JoAnn told her that she bet a pack of cigarettes that she will come out and have some money. She asked where was Bell and I told her that Bell had left. She asked if Bell was coming back and I said, "Yes." JoAnn then left and went back to Leroy's apartment and got some cookies then JoAnn left. Ten minutes later, Leroy came and asked was Bell back yet and I said, "No," and he said she promise him she would be back. Then Tony came and went to Leroy's apartment and stayed for about 5 to 10 minutes. Tony came to my apartment and asked me for a cigarette. I told him I only had a few, so I told George to give him a cigarette so there would be no trouble. So he gave Tony a cigarette and Tony asked George where did he work and George said the Civic Center.

Tony then left and went back to Leroy's apartment and they talked for 10 minutes. Then Leroy and Tony walked into my apartment and I told Leroy not to have the gun in there cause someone might get hurt. He said it wasn't loaded. Leroy pointed the gun at George Sparks and the gun went off. George threw his left hand up and fell to the floor. I got down to the floor to see if George was all right but seen the blood an' George was dead and Tony said to Leroy, "Are you going to get rid of her?" Leroy said, "No," and I said, "Please don't hurt me and my baby." Tony told me to shut up. Then Tony told Leroy to give him the gun and he will do away with me. Leroy said, "No." Then Tony said to get the baby and come on, so I asked where was I going and Tony said none of my business. Then he told me I was going to Tony's apartment. Tony opened his door and pushed me in. I tried to avoid it but Leroy held the gun at my back and I knew that I didn't have any choice. So with my baby in my arm I went in. Leroy said, "Lay the baby down on the bed," so I did. I had to use the bathroom but before I got to the bathroom I heard the police. Tony had left to go to bootleg house to get some wine. The police was knocking at the door, they yelled to open it or they will kick it in. When they said that, Leroy fired through the door and missed a police officer. Then I heard a shot fired through the window and I ducked out of the way. Leroy told them that they almost shot me, so the police said, "If you don't shoot at us, we won't shoot at you." Leroy then put my baby up to the window and told them that there was a baby in there. So the police didn't shoot but Leroy said to shoot and I said, "No, my baby is in the window." So the police didn't shoot anymore. My baby was crying and Leroy told me to quiet the baby so I did.

While we were in the apartment, Leroy was thinking of a way to escape, but he knew if he would try he was going to be shot. So he didn't try to escape any more. He told the police to go and get his ex-wife Jenifer. He said he wanted to talk to her then he would give me and the baby up and shoot her and hisself. The police did get her but she refused to talk to him. So he told the police to send him a cigarette and he would think about giving up, but he didn't the first time. He said if he had a cigarette, he would let the baby go and keep me. I asked him was he serious and he shook his head no. Then he said he would tie the gun to my baby's head and I said, "Please don't hurt my baby." While the police were at the door, I asked for a pain pill 'cause I was having slight pains. They slipped a pill through the door.

Then Leroy and I were talking and he asked for a cigarette and he would think about setting us free. They sent a cigarette through the door and I had promised Leroy I would tell and he told me to stick up for him 'cause he saved my life. So I lied to him and told him that I would lie, but deep inside me I couldn't tell no lie 'cause I would get in trouble. So Leroy says he gives up and as he unloaded the gun and was getting ready to throw it out the window, I made my way to the door and moved the couch and dresser from the door. I unlocked the door and I walked out with my baby and Leroy followed me. I went to the Public Safety Building and the baby went to the hospital. They cuffed Leroy and took him to the Public Safety Building. They questioned me. I told them what happened and all that I seened. They took me from the Public Safety Building to my mother's house. They said to be at court Tuesday morning at 10:00 and testify. That is the whole story.

Beverly Ann Jones

As in any case, the statements of those involved often differ as the point of view of the participant changes. It is as if one were looking at the same incident through constantly changing lenses which distort and highlight differing aspects of the same scene. Here is the statement made by Beverly Ann Jones, Earline's sister Bell. She says:

On Thursday the 24th of February 1977, at around 11:20 P.M. I got at Earline Jones' house, located in an apartment on the second floor of 160 South Avenue. Earline answered the door. I went in and saw George Sparks and Earline's baby Clint in the front room. After sitting down for a few minutes I asked Earline where Tony was? She said Tony was gone, he was very upset. So

I asked where Leroy was? She told me that he was sitting home waiting for Tony. I asked why. She said, "Because he's very mad and upset for what Tony did." I asked, "What did he do?" She said, "He broked in Leroy's house and took his money." We all were watching television and talking about food. Earline got up and took a frozen chicken out and put it in water. She asked me to go over to Leroy's house and get a knife to cut the chicken with.

It was around 11:35 P.M. when I walked next door to Leroy's apartment. Leroy answered the door. I walked into the kitchen and said," E. J. (Earline Jones), wants a knife." I don't know when E. J. walked in but she was standing in the doorway. Leroy said to E. J., "All I have is a case knife (butter knife)." Earline took the knife and left.

I went into the front room and sat down. I noticed a rifle lying down on the chair. I asked Leroy what he had the gun for and was it real. He said, "Yea it's real. I'm gonna kill Tony." I asked him, "What for?" He told me that Tony had broke into his house and got his money. Leroy stood up and took off his shirt, and kept looking out the window. He said, "Come on I got to rap with you." We got up and went into his bedroom and sat on the bed. Leroy had brought the gun which was on the chair into the room. He pulled something on the gun and took a gold bullet out and showed it to me. He then put the bullet back and leaned the gun up against the wall. Leroy sat down on the bed with me. He took off my boots and started taking off my shirt. I was scared and I told him not to do that, as I had to go. Leroy continued until he had taken off my shirt and bra, and had put them in his suitcase. He tried to pull my pants off but only got them off one leg. Leroy began to try and get his penis in me but I stopped him by putting my hand down there. I was really afraid of Leroy because of the gun. The whole time he was undressing me and grabbing me I told him that I had to go, but I'd be back. Actually if I got free I was not going to come back. I heard E. J. knocking on Leroy's door saying Bobby's coming, (Bobby Sparks, brother to George Sparks the murder victim). I told Leroy that I really had to go as Bobby was my main man. Leroy let me up and I got dressed. Leroy asked me if I wanted any money, and I said, "No." I asked if I could have some cookies. He gave me a couple and I started to leave. Before I got out of the house Leroy said, "Wait a minute! I'll be at E. J.'s in 15 minutes."

I returned to E. J.'s apartment and found that besides E. J., George, the baby and a girl named JoAnn was there. JoAnn said to me, "You did all that and didn't get a dollar?" So I told her no, because I didn't do nothing. JoAnn brought up the subject of betting me that if she was to go over to Leroy's house that she'd get a dollar. I told her I'd bet a pack of cigarettes that if she went over there she wouldn't get anything. JoAnn left and went to Leroy's. My sister, E. J., said Bobby was looking for me. I said, "Oh," and mentioned that I was going downstairs to catch some air. When I got downstairs I ran to my apartment on Kirk Avenue. At around 7:30 A.M. the 25th of February 1977, I walked over to my family's house. My mother said to me, "I thought you were going to stay over to E. J.'s." I told her that I couldn't because I got scared. My mother told me that at about 3:00 A.M. she had heard on the news that a person got shot in an apartment where E. J. lived. She also said that JoAnn had come over about the same time and told her that E. J. was in bad trouble and needed some help. Sometime around 9:00 A.M. I went over to South Avenue with E. J.'s nurse and stood in the crowd and watched what was going on. At around 4:00 P.M. I was picked up by a couple of police investigators and brought to the Criminal Investigation Division of the Public Safety Building to make a statement as to what I had seen and done. I told the police that I was willing to make such a statement. While in the Criminal Investigation Division I was asked to look at a gun. The investigators showed me a gun and asked me if it looked like the gun Leroy had. I told them that it looked just like the gun Leroy had. Being the same color and size as the rifle at Leroy's.

Thomas (Tony) Lee

Tony tells quite a different story of his involvement than that told by Earline Jones. As we shall see, these differences go beyond the obvious motivations of exculpation. Tony says:

Today, Friday, February 25th 1977, I arrive home at my apartment at about 2:00 A.M. and I went up to apartment #5 which is the apartment of Leroy Cotton. I knocked on the door of Leroy's apartment and Leroy said, "Come in." When I entered Leroy's apartment I saw him sitting by the window in a chair with a rifle in his lap. I began to talk to Leroy and he was acting very violent and he was making threats about other people. After listening to Leroy talk like he was, I was frightened and I made an excuse to leave the apartment by saying that I wanted to get a cigarette from the apartment next door. I went to apartment #6, which is the apartment of a lady named E. J., and I knocked on the door and she let me in. When I entered E. J.'s apartment there was a man in the apartment with her named Sparks and E. J.'s baby was lying on the couch. I asked E. J. for a cigarette and she said she only have two, and I said could I have one and she gave me a Newport cigarette. At this time, which was about 2:15 A.M. Leroy walked into the apartment, with his rifle. Leroy told Sparks to turn around because Sparks had his back to him. When Sparks turned around Leroy shot him once in the head with this rifle and Sparks fell to the floor. Leroy said, "See if he is dead," and I turned him over and said, "He is gone." When I turned Sparks over I observed that he had a head wound and he was bleeding from the head.

Leroy then said, "Let's go over here," and he pointed at my apartment with the rifle, and all four of us went into my apartment which is apartment #7. After we were in my apartment I knew that I had to cause some kind of diversion to get out so I went to the door and pretended to hear something outside the door and, while I was pretending to hear something, I was unlocking the door. After I managed to get the door unlocked, Leroy said, "Where are you going," and I said, "No where," and I said, "I thought I heard someone coming." Leroy started talking to the girl and I knew his attention was off me and at this time I ran out the door and this is the last time I saw Leroy or the baby or E. J. I ran out of the house and I kept running until I got to Tallman and South Avenue and I saw a police car at the corner, and I told the policeman what had happened. I was asked to come to the Public Safety Building where I am making this statement. While at the Criminal Investigation Office, I was shown a photograph of a man and I was told that the man's name is George Sparks III, and I wish to state that this is positively the same man that I saw Leroy Cotton shoot on February 25th 1977.

Officer Daniel Boyle

The investigation reports filed by the responding officers of the Syracuse Police Department relate the first police responses. Officer Daniel Boyle filed the following report:

On 25 February 1977, at approximately 0219 hours while working car #59, this officer observed a black male running south in the 100 block of South Avenue, while I was parked at the traffic light at the corner of South and Tallman. I then called to this man (later identified as Thomas Lee) and asked him what the problem was. Thomas Lee (nicknamed Tony) said that he had just witnessed a shooting and murder and then continued to run west on Tallman Street. This officer then placed Lee in the rear of Car #59 and asked him where he had seen the shooting. Lee stated that it happened at 160 South Avenue in apartment #6, and that the suspect was named Leroy Cotton and was in apartment #7 with the weapon. This officer then notified the dispatcher to send a couple of officers to 160 South Avenue on a possible shooting as I proceeded to the scene. When I arrived I told Thomas Lee to stay in the police car while I went to the front door of 160 South Avenue.

Other officers then arrived on the scene at this time which included P.O. Pallotta, P.O. Bland, P.O. McLaughlin, Inv. Venton, Sgt. Mumford, and Lt. Galvin. We then proceeded to the second floor of 160 South Avenue, apartment #6, where the victim was supposed to be in this shooting. Upon knocking and no response being given, the door was kicked in by Officer Bland. When the door to apartment #6 was opened, a black male was found laying on the floor of what appeared to be the kitchen area. Blood was coming from this man's head at which time first aid was administered. Eastern Ambulance then arrived on the scene at which time the victim of the shooting (later identified as being George Sparks) showed no signs of life.

We then went across the hall to apartment #7 where the suspect (Cotton) was supposed to be. We knocked on the door and identified ourselves as police officers. A male then yelled through the door that he would not open the door. A few minutes later a shot came from inside apartment #7 out through the hall door almost striking Officer Pallotta and Sgt. Mumford who were standing on the side of the door. The man inside (Cotton) also stated that a female (Ms. Jones) and her young daughter were inside with him. The premises were surrounded by other officers responding. Command personnel were notified and came to the scene. Lt. Galvin attempted to talk the suspect out of the apartment while Officers Pallotta, Danes, Sgt. Mumford, Sgt. Burns and this officer stood by to assist. At approximately 0715 hours, I was relieved at the scene while the suspect was still held up in the apartment. I then came to CID for a statement.

Sgt. Timothy Mumford

Sgt. Timothy Mumford describes his initial response as follows:

On 25 February 1977, while assigned to car #26, responded to a homicide at 160 South Avenue. Upon arrival with other units of the SPD, was informed that a body had been found in one of the apartments, the victim of an apparent homicide. The complaint stated that the suspect was in apartment #7, and that he had a gun. Along with P.O. Pallotta and Sgt. Buske, Lt. J. Galvin pounded on the door, without results. After a period of a few minutes the residents of the apartment responded stating that they wished to see our ID. While this conversation was taking place, the suspect, Leroy Cotton, shot through the closed door. Wood chips from the shot struck this writer and P.O. Pallotta in the face, causing minor wounds.

At this point the suspect fired again, this time through an outside window. Went to the roof, covering the first floor rear porch. Walked along the roof until coming to one of the apartment windows. At this point, suspect stuck the barrel of the rifle out the window, and fired one round. This writer fired one round from his service weapon and returned to the rear of the roof. The suspect closed and locked the window. Returned to the hallway of the second floor and assisted Lt. Galvin while he attempted to talk the suspect out of the apartment. In the apartment with the suspect was a mother and her child.

At 0230 hours, I (Dr. Miron) received a telephone call at my home asking me to go to the scene to assist the police department. When I arrived, the street was already beginning to fill with the curious despite the early hour. The subject was holed up in a second floor apartment of the two-story frame house. The windows of the apartment faced the back and side of the house. From the side window, it was obvious that the perpetrator could see all of the police activity at the south end of the block. All of the units still had their emergency lights flashing. As we entered from the south, through the outer barricade perimeter which had been established, it became clear that we would be crossing directly through the possible line of fire from the side window. So warned, we turned back to approach from the north end of the street. After going around the block and finally stopping just short of the house on the blind side of the apartment, I got out of the car to walk over to the Chief. As yet, no command post had been established and our initial conference was conducted in the middle of the street.

After a brief conversation, we entered the house through the front door facing on South Avenue, and passed through a small foyer to the first floor landing. The other apartments had already been cleared. An old and creaking set of stairs led up to the barricaded apartment just off the second floor landing. The side wall of the apartment faced the stairs and was paper thin in construction. The door to the apartment faced the wall of the apartment in which the body of George Sparks still lay dead in a small pool of blood. Lt. James Galvin, duty officer on the 12 to 8 shift was crouched at the top of the stairs talking to the subject through the door of the apartment. I crouched down beside Galvin, half lying on the floor. Sparks' body was no more than five feet away from us. The second floor was uncomfortably hot and someone propped open the windows at either end of the hall in an effort to make it more comfortable.

Sometime later the heat emanating from the apartment in which Cotton had turned on the oven, posed another practical problem as the body of Sparks began to ripen. I estimate that there were at least six officers positioned at either end of the hallway and another eight to ten people milling about the stairway and the lower landing. At one point even the fire marshal put in an appearance. Every move on the stairs or in the hallway could be heard through the thin walls. Lt. Galvin and I had never met, but he knew of me. He quickly briefed me on what had transpired up to that time. At this point, Cotton was most concerned that the police might try to break into the apartment. The woman hostage, Ms. Jones, kept screaming for the police to get away from the door. Galvin calmly and repeatedly assured Cotton that so long as he didn't make any aggressive moves, the police would not attempt to gain entrance or shoot at him. Cotton had positioned himself in the apartment well away from the door so that both he and Galvin had to raise their voices somewhat to be heard.

As the day wore on, the strain of trying to catch what Cotton was saying significantly added to the fatigue everyone began to feel. It was not until at least six hours into the crisis that a transmitter microphone was placed at the door so that others not immediately beside the door could receive and record the transmission over a closed radio fre- quency. Before this, a portable tape recorder had been turned on with its microphone lying on the floor beside Galvin and me. I recall looking at the tape recorder at one point to realize that I had forgotten to flip the cassette long after the tape had come to the end and then promptly forgot it again in the press of the negotiations.

The local FBI agents suggested that the communications would be more personalized if we could rig up a phone line between Cotton and

Galvin. I argued against the plan on the grounds that 1) it might appear to be an aggrandizing concession to Cotton's importance. 2) It would create a logistic problem in getting the phone into Cotton, requiring either that he unbarricade the door or that it be ferried up through the window which was covered by a nailed-on screen. Either move, it seemed to me, would considerably complicate the negotiations and might be interpreted by Cotton as a subterfuge to allow the S.W.A.T. team a clear shot at him. 3) By forcing Cotton to speak up we were increasing his discomfort and energy expenditure closer to the time when he would find it easier just to give up. 4) Cotton could discontinue the negotiations unilaterally by simply putting down the phone once that link became the primary channel of communication.

The decision not to try to use a phone line may or may not have been correct. It was a difficult decision to reach and is typical of the tactical decisions which must constantly be made in such situations. In the end, I put it to Lt. Galvin as a decision which I felt he was in the best position to make. If he thought that talking through the door was not hindering his attempts to negotiate with Cotton, I felt that we should not risk the complication the advantage of possibly developing greater rapport might provide. As it developed, the suggestion was again repeated later on when we seemed to have reached the point in the negotiations where no new ground was being made. At that point, I suggested again to Lt. Galvin, that if he felt it proper, he might ask Cotton whether Cotton would like to talk over a phone "to make things easier." Phrased in this positive manner, Lt. Galvin, himself, anxious for some way out of the impasse, made the suggestion to Cotton. This point is important. During such a crisis even the smallest decisions carry risky implications should they be wrong. Someone will have to account for his actions after the crisis is over.

This particular hostage situation was complicated by other, related factors which should be discussed. My presence as "an advisor" at Lt. Galvin's shoulder, "the doctor" who routinely teaches crisis procedures, could have made his task intolerable. It was vital that Lt. Galvin, who in my judgment was the perfect man for the job, be allowed to use his own instincts and judgments. He needed to feel the confidence that what he thought best was right. My presence was to be one of support, available for discussion, but that this was not a problem in psychology so much as it was a law enforcement operation. Thus, in all of my discussions with Galvin, I would periodically remind him that he was in the best position to know what he could and couldn't do and that he was **Lieutenant** Galvin, eminently well-trained in law enforcement. If Lt. Galvin had been someone else, someone who was rigid and uncompromising in his image of what law enforcement should mean, the tactic would have clearly been inappropriate. The gods smiled when the incident happened to occur on Galvin's shift. What do you do when there aren't any Galvins around? What happens if the responding officer believes that negotiation panders to criminals? You relieve him.

But suppose the first man at the scene is the last man you would have picked but nonetheless has established effective communications which look like they are going well? You work with him. As with everything else in a crisis, you use what is at hand to the maximum advantage. The difficulty is that if you relieve someone who has already started negotiations, you have clearly indicated to the perpetrator that there is someone out there who has command authority and who has the power to do what he, the perpetrator, wants. You can try to relieve an ineffective communicator by saying that his shift is up and that he had to go home, but you'd better make sure that the story holds up. In one New York City incident, it tooks hours to locate the officer who had begun negotiations and had been relieved. The subject insisted that he wouldn't talk to anyone else. It is far better to have a departmental procedure which mandates that the responding officer in such a situation should wait for the hostage negotiation team to get to the scene to begin negotiations and to use the time to begin clearing the area and establishing the perimeters.

Cotton's response to the suggestion of a phone was dramatic. He was dumbfounded. He had not had a phone. Getting a phone is a complicated matter which requires credit, waiting periods and bureaucratic hassle. Here were the police saying they could get one right now and it would be his alone. Cotton gained 12 inches in stature, and I was convinced that we had made a mistake. We had confirmed his importance. Up to this time we had successfully fended off his demands for (1) a plane to fly him to Cuba, (2) amnesty, (3) the Chief of Police, (4) his former wife and (5) cigarettes. In each instance, Lt. Galvin had neatly pointed out the difficulties, stalled or changed the subject. Cotton was beginning to feel like the ordinary guy he knew himself to be. We had the Chief supposedly in Albany, a good three-hour ride from Syracuse, trying to get a car. After more than three hours had passed and Cotton asked again where the hell the Chief was, Galvin instinctively responded with the best possible reply: "Hell, I don't know, he's probably shacked up somewhere." And Cotton never raised the subject again. Had I been talking with him, I probably would have said something stupid like, "Maybe he has a flat tire." Galvin and I differ in one very essential ingredient, he is streetwise.

For Cotton, Galvin's response made good sense. As for Cotton's former wife, Galvin had replied that she (1) was scared to come up, and (2) that he couldn't allow anyone to be put into danger, that it was against departmental policy. The plane to Cuba was passed off as more a fancy than a real demand, and was simply ignored by changing the subject. The amnesty issue provided an essential lever in the negotiations. Cotton was well aware of the Kiritsis incident. He could not have named the perpetrator or his victim, but he knew that someone had negotiated for amnesty in such a situation and that the cops had betrayed the fellow. He raised the issue repeatedly. Galvin kept trying to tell Cotton that about all we had on him was a charge of firing a weapon in the city limits and what was the big deal. In point of fact, if one were to take Cotton's account of what had happened, there would be little beyond a series of minor violations on which he could be held. Cotton represented that Thomas Lee, in fact, shot Sparks and that he, the baby and Ms. Jones had barricaded themselves in the apartment out of fear that Lee would shoot them. He declared that he had no idea that it was the police who had responded to the call and that he had shot at them in self-defense. Ms. Jones, at Cotton's prodding, fully confirmed this account and indicated that she was ready to swear to its truthfulness.

In fact, after the incident, her first statement to the police largely followed this line. It was not until four days later that she wrote the modified statement given at the beginning of this chapter. Galvin kept pointing out that Cotton's best witness was right in there with him and that if any harm befell her, he would lose his best ally. Galvin pointed out that if Cotton gave up now, he could still make the afternoon arraignment and be out on bail within hours. All of Cotton's previous experience with the law, and he had had his share, certainly confirmed the truthfulness of the ease with which offenders seem to get out of jail. Further, Galvin argued that they couldn't hold Lee if Cotton didn't come down to the station and make his statement. There were, of course, numerous discrepancies in Cotton's story, but Galvin, without declaring that he believed him, kept repeating that "if" what he said were true, the authorities could only book him for firing his gun. As Cotton kept telling his story, continually encouraged by Galvin, confirmed by Ms. Jones, one could sense that Cotton was beginning to believe himself.

We studiously avoided even an indirect mention of the homicide, and Cotton never raised the issue. The human mind works in peculiar ways. If you cut the skin and begin to bleed, the blood quickly coagulates to close the wound. If you commit an act which has gotten you in trouble, the mind tries to blot out your recognition of that act. In a very short time you can actually convince yourself that it never happened or at least that it didn't happen the way it did. How many times have you had an argument with someone and said some things you wish you hadn't only to find that a few days later you can't remember that you said them at all? The process is known as "repression," and just as with clotting it occurs without your even being aware of it.

When Cotton wasn't elaborating on his story, he would return to his demands, and particularly that he wanted his former wife brought to him. I had been given copies of Cotton's rap sheet and the divorce decree. Cotton's previous arrests had been on various forms of assault charges, but none of them had resulted in any serious injuries. Cotton was reputed to carry his rifle with him on many occasions. There was a report that he had tried to trade in his .22 for a 12-gauge shotgun just a few days earlier. I had talked at some length to his former wife in one of my trips back downstairs shortly after my arrival. She had indicated that Cotton had often threatened to kill her, almost always when he was drunk, but beyond slapping her around some, he had never seriously harmed her. The divorce action related a long history of verbal and physical abuse. Two days earlier, the wife reported to me, Cotton had followed their 10-year-old son home from school and had tried to beat him up. Cotton was obviously a violent man, but his courage appeared to come in bottles. His targets were chosen carefully from among the relatively helpless. But we also knew that Cotton had been drinking at the time Sparks was shot.

It was clear that bringing Cotton's former wife to him would be an invitation to murder at worst, but more likely, just the audience which Cotton might want to commit suicide in front of. Very early on, I had come to the conclusion that suicide was, in fact, the most likely danger we had to deal with. Right or wrong, I had concluded that his hostages were safe so long as Cotton was not pushed into action. On a number of occasions, Cotton had declared that he was "a born loser," and that as a black he had never "had a chance." Thus, it became important to keep his hopes up and to prevent him from falling into depression. At a number of points in the negotiations, I warned Galvin to change the subject as I thought I saw Cotton start into depression. We wanted just enough depression to convince him to give up but not so much that he would prefer suicide. The best strategy was to play the lead of the story he offered for what had happened and to treat the negotiations both as a potential suicide and as a hostage situation. Just before Cotton surrendered, this suspicion was dramatically confirmed. Sgt. Mumford reported that he saw Cotton briefly place the muzzle of his gun into his mouth. I believe that Cotton's requests for cigarettes and, later, for a pint of vodka, were the requests of a man seriously considering suicide.

At the time, we had no idea that cigarettes had played so important a part in the actions of the principals just before the shooting. What we did know is that Cotton desperately wanted a smoke. For hours, Galvin had successfully put off his requests by changing the subject or pointing out that there was no way to get cigarettes in to him unless Cotton opened the door. As it developed, a cigarette became the principal negotiating tool. One cigarette almost, ridiculously, became worth everything. So long as the bargaining was over a cigarette, it was clear that all of Cotton's other demands looked monumental compared to something so trivial. If he couldn't get the concession of a smoke, how was he to even consider having the cops bring his wife to him? That one cigarette became the whole ball game; to get it, he would have to give up. As to the vodka, Galvin passed over the request as absurd with the comment, "Now where the hell am I going to get any vodka at this time of the morning." Cotton's return suggestion was that he go by the bootlegger's place for it, to which Galvin snorted, "He's not gonna sell anything to me, for cripes sake." To which Cotton laughingly responded, "Hell, man, he probably give it you fer nuthin'." At this point, one of the officials whispered in my ear that we should do it and put some knockout drops into it. I felt that such a plan would be too complicated and risky, explaining that Cotton might give it to the baby or the woman to test, or that he might detect the drug before it had time to take effect.

Although there was never any question that we would not accede to Cotton's request to have his former wife brought to him, his demand provided considerable insight into his latent problems. The fact that Cotton considered his former wife to be the principal audience for whatever he was contemplating meant that she was probably the primary target of his anger and resentment. Consequently, we were able to use this insight in our negotiations by encouraging him to blame his difficulties on her. But we pointed out that he would never have the satisfaction of his telling her what a mess she had caused if something were to happen to him. If he gave up, we would bring her down to the station so that he could confront her directly. It was not his hostages which should be punished, but his wife who had left him and made him feel less than the man he was. She had gotten him into this jam, and now she would have to feel sorry for what she had done. Let me hasten to point out that none of these things were said in so blatant a way. What we did was plant the seeds of this reasoning for Cotton himself to let flower. What we said were things like, "If your wife hadn't left you, you probably wouldn't be in this mess, isn't that right?" "Well, we'll certainly want to bring your wife down to the station when we take your statement." "We can't let your wife come up here. It's against regulations to put any civilian in danger, but you can see her down at the station after you give up. We'll make sure of that."

Cotton did not have enough insight into his own problems to have realized what was really making him so angry. If he had had such insight, he would not have been in this jam to begin with. His behavior that entire evening had been completely expressive. He was demonstrating to the entire world that he was a man and that no "dumb broad" was going to walk out on him. Much later on, this same key prompted offering that he would not be handcuffed when he gave up so that he could "walk out like a man." Looking back on this with the advantage of hindsight, I now believe this suggestion might have been another mistake. I think that it might have been more satisfying for him to have thought he would be handcuffed so that he would believe that his wife would see him shackled. His desire to have his wife feel guilty might have made the humiliation more like a badge of honor given to the suffering hero he wanted to appear as. Of course, he **was** handcuffed the instant he surrendered so that, in fact, the outcome was the same. On the positive side, however, the suggestion of not using handcuffs at least served to implicitly confirm the acceptance of the story he had related of his innocence.

As the negotiations progressed, Cotton's need for a smoke had gotten to the point where it became reasonable to suggest that he trade the baby for a cigarette. Incredible as it seems, we entered into a period in which we bargained over just how many cigarettes would be exchanged for the baby. Cotton started out at a pack and we bargained him down to two. Writing this now, I fully appreciate how calloused this appears to be. But those few cigarettes in this crisis, had taken on a symbolic value far in excess of the tobacco involved. Further, we had no guarantee whatsoever that Cotton would keep his end of the bargain. If we gave him all the cigarettes he wanted, we would have lost one of our primary bargaining tools.

As it turned out, we did not get the baby. After we passed the two cigarettes through a crack in the door, we started to make arrangements for Ms. Jones to hand the baby out. She balked. She said that she didn't want her baby taken away from her. We argued that we would get her mother or a nurse to take care of it and that the baby would be far better off out of there. Ms. Jones continued to refuse. As we learned later from her statement, she contends that it was Cotton who prevented her from releasing the baby. At the time, however, we had no knowledge of this and continued to try to reassure her.

We sent out word to find the mother and this resulted in one of our most intense embarrassments. Word came back that they had the mother, a Mrs. _____, downstairs. We passed this along to Earline so that she would know the baby would be in good hands. Her reply was that she knew no such person, and that it certainly wasn't her mother. I could nearly taste the egg on our faces. We did finally get the mother's name straight, but the initiative had already been lost. It was my judgment, however, that the baby was not in any danger. In fact, we now had another lever to use against Cotton. We pointed out to Cotton that he had broken his promise. He kept insisting that it was not him but her who refused to let the baby out, but nonetheless we let him know that he had promised the baby's release. Ms. Jones **did not** at any time that we could hear, attempt to persuade Cotton. Throughout the siege, in fact, she continually supported Cotton's story and did not importune him for her or her baby's release. Why? The probable explanation is that she had fully undergone the effects of the Stockholm Effect.

She was his ally working with him against the greater fear she felt toward the police outside. It would have helped us if she had tried to convince Cotton to give up or to at least release her or her baby. Under the influence of the effect, however, in her mind her survival depended upon her full cooperation with Cotton. He had the gun and appeared to be in complete charge of the situation; we were being helplessly held at bay. Who would appear the more powerful? At the last moment just before Cotton surrendered, Sergeant Mumford peering through the crack in the door reported to us that he saw the two of them necking! It is easy to argue that all of this only indicates that Ms. Jones was no victim at all, that she was a co-conspirator right from the beginning. I believe such interpretations to be wrong. It is the same interpretation which many offered for Patty Hearst's bizarre behavior. It was wrong there and it would be wrong here. Ms. Jones and her baby **were** hostages. They **were** in danger. It could have turned out differently, there was no one present who even considered otherwise.

Under the interpretation, however, that suicide was the more likely outcome of this crisis, it became less critically urgent that we secure the release of the hostages. The baby had been peacefully sleeping for more than 10 hours and showed no signs of distress. Ms. Jones was calm and, despite her pregnancy, clearly not in any pain or discomfort. The police had phoned the physician listed on a prescription found in Earline's apartment. He had indicated that she did not really require any medication and was in good health. The prescription was for Darvon, a mild analgesic. Nonetheless, we seized upon this medication as a device for testing Cotton's concern for his hostage. After telling Ms. Jones that she should really have the medicine her doctor had prescribed, we asked Cotton if we were to pass it through the door would he see that she got it. When he agreed, we slipped one pill through a crack. Galvin made a big show of making sure that Earline had taken the pill and that Cotton had done a really good thing in giving her her medicine.

Later, we tried to establish the same gesture for the baby. Galvin asked Earline whether the baby needed milk even though it was clear that the infant was fast asleep. Interestingly enough, milk was also being discussed outside. The media trying to drum up some excitement in what otherwise was getting rather dull, started to pointedly ask their viewers why the police were not more concerned about getting the baby some milk. They correctly reported that they had not seen anyone carrying any milk into the house. We got the report upstairs, and we arranged to send a man out to buy the biggest bottle of milk he could find and bring it back as ostentiously as he could for us to drink.

Media

Let's talk about the media. Bluntly put, they and their influence can be downright dangerous. There is no single influence in such situations which has a greater impact, barring the perpetrator himself, than the media. These situations make or break politicians depending on how the media choose to report them. The media are powerful and they are at some pains to point that out to you. I am told that one of the ranking officials, who was, in fact, out of town, is reported to have said that he didn't want anything to happen until he got back. When he arrived at the scene, the Chief asked me to come downstairs to brief him on what was happening and what I thought our chances were. Much impressed by the company I was in, I began to lay out the tactics in some detail we were so far successfully employing. I had been talking for perhaps three or four minutes, when there was a sudden rush of men just at the top of the stairs. I turned to see all of the officers with their guns drawn, crouched in two-fisted firing positions. (Cotton, throughout the negotiations, had been periodically making sudden aggressive moves toward the barricaded door and had been racking the bolt of his rifle over and over again. I couldn't tell what might have happened, but the air was suddenly charged with the tension that falls just before an explosion.) I stopped mid-sentence, incredibly said excuse me, and dashed for the stairs to get back to Galvin. It turned out to be a false alarm and we went back to calming Cotton down. Nevertheless, it turns out that this false alarm was a stroke of incredible luck. For I am told that soon afterward, the city official went before the television cameras to repeat, including his own psychological elaborations, what had just been told him. None of this, had Cotton heard it, would have done us one iota of good.

Fortunately, Cotton had neither television nor radio in the apartment. Even if he had, the order had been put out to cut the power if we heard the incident played back to us via the media from inside the apartment. But what of the 20 other guys glued to their screens with whom we would have to negotiate next week? It is also obvious that this book itself is part of the media, even though less accessible than an on-the-spot interview, and despite the fact that it is designed for law enforcement officers. We all share in the responsibility. There clearly should be limits on what is said and when. In one of my trips to report to the command post, a reporter asked me for an interview and I told him I would be happy to cooperate next week, but that right now it was inappropriate.

During the Hanafi incident, CBS News called me from New York to ask me my opinion of what was going on. It took me half an hour to explain why I chose to say, "No comment." During the search for Patty Hearst, CBS News ferreted me out in phone call after phone call, from where I was hiding to avoid them. I did appear on national TV, but only after I had carefully rehearsed myself for a statement I thought might assist the negotiations for Patty's release. In incident after incident, the great and the not-so-great have chosen to use these emergencies as vehicles for their own exposure. Is it any wonder that the perpetrator wants some for himself? After Cotton surrendered, the city official emerged from the house carrying the infant cradled in his arms. *The New York Times* carried the picture. Lt. Galvin was not in the picture because he was still upstairs busy wiping the sweat from his brow. I am **not** saying that law enforcement officers or anyone else should pretend to false modesty of faceless anonymity. There are few enough rewards for those in law enforcement. What I am saying is that what one says to the media must be part of the solution, not part of the problem.

The Surrender

When the negotiations with Cotton had come to the point of the suggestion that we install a direct phone line with him, his reaction indicated that he considered it a concession to his importance and, as I said, I considered it a mistake. Nonetheless, one can even use one's mistakes effectively. We discarded the idea, and when Cotton asked what was happening about the phone, Galvin said they were having trouble getting it rigged up. Cotton understood this perfectly. It served to confirm his impression that nothing could be achieved easily, that problems surrounded him like a plague, and that Galvin had no flying carpet that would magically fly him out of there. The world, for Cotton, was back to normal – just a set of problems. But now, Galvin could solve Cotton's problem in the way everybody knew it had to come to sooner or later. The ordinary, undramatic way of walking off to jail. No gadgets, no trumpets blaring, just another trip to the Public Safety Building. The problem now was to get Cotton to move off the dime. To start his feet moving in the right direction.

Everyone in that hallway could sense that the moment was at hand. We had to grab the moment now before it slipped away from us again. Cotton had set a deadline for himself of 10 A.M. for some purpose he never told us. I believed it to be for his suicide, and we had let the deadline go by without comment. Now, six hours later, we reminded him of the deadline for making the late afternoon arraignment, and told him he had better hurry or he'd have to wait for tomorrow's court. He asked for a cigarette, promising to come out if we gave him one. Galvin got stubborn and continued to stall. I practically jumped up and down in my anguish that the critical moment would pass and we would be back to a standoff of wills. I madly gestured for Galvin to give him a cigarette. Now we could afford the concession. The Lieutenant finally did. But then I urged that he keep reminding Cotton that he had better hurry and to finish the smoke on the way down.

At this point things were moving very fast in contrast to the leisurely pace of the negotiations during the previous 13 hours. Galvin directed Cotton to throw his gun out the window and to let Ms. Jones and the baby out first. Galvin carefully instructed Cotton to empty the weapon and to throw it out butt first. He made a huge show of shouting loudly that Cotton was coming to the window to throw out his gun and that the men were to hold their fire, the order, of course, having been passed quietly down the line well before this. As Galvin shouted in his best stage voice of command authority, he could hardly repress the giggle of relief he felt. Cotton was not out yet, but we all knew it was over. The gun was thrown clear and Ms. Jones began moving the furniture from the barricaded door. As she emerged Cotton was right behind her, still smoking his cigarette. That is the last I saw of him. As he was hustled out, all of us whooped and laughed in uncontainable joy. Backs were patted, hands were shaken again and again. It looked like a Boy Scout picnic in that narrow hallway.

The Aftermath

Suddenly, I was dog-tired and all jangled nerves. Now there was no need to keep my cool and I wanted to get out of there and away as fast as I could. I could hear the crowds outside cheering the officials as they emerged with the infant. The local FBI agent offered me a ride home and I gratefully accepted. It was a beautiful day. As we walked up the street toward the barricades restraining the crowds of onlookers and the hot dog stands that had been set up to feed them, I suddenly became deeply depressed. I stopped dead in my tracks to watch a youth vault the barricade and start running screaming toward the secured house before he was wrestled to the ground by two officers. I watched a news camera team rush by me loaded down with their equipment, and one of them trip and fall head over heels into the gutter. I was dumbfounded. I stood there in shock, unable to comprehend any of this. As they dragged the youth off, I asked myself if I might see him again in some seedy apartment house threatening to kill some other hostage. I looked down at my badly soiled jacket, caked with the dirt of the floor I had lain on for thirteen and a half hours and thanked God that I could go home — that it was over and that it had turned out all right.

3 / The Kiritsis Case

It was a chilling five degrees in Indianapolis the day Anthony Kiritsis decided that he had had enough of the Meridian Mortgage Company. Kiritsis had borrowed $130,000 from the company three years earlier to purchase a 17-acre tract on which he had planned to build a shopping center. The loan was to fall due at the end of the month. Richard Hall, an executive of the mortgage company, had repeatedly refused to extend the deadline. Kiritsis contended that Hall had been responsible for dissuading several potential lessees from locating on his property. With no hope of developing the property, Kiritsis faced foreclosure and bankruptcy.

Anthony was a 44-year-old former West Point gun instructor who was well acquainted with firearms and explosives. Several days before he marched into the office of Richard Hall, he had purchased 25 sticks of dynamite. Armed with a sawed-off shotgun which he strapped around Hall's neck, Kiritsis marched his victim in shirt sleeves out onto the street. Followed by news cameras as he wandered toward the Indiana Statehouse in downtown Indianapolis, Kiritsis shouted that Hall "had left me out in the cold and now I'm going to put you out in the cold and kill you." At the steps of the State House, Kiritsis commandeered a city police car and ordered Hall to drive to Kiritsis' apartment. And so began a 63-hour siege.

In the world of hostage-taking, this incident marked a critical point which has had a significant impact upon the course of subsequent negotiations. Post-Kiritsis, we have had to take into account the problem of immunity in negotiating with the perpetrator and its related problem of the credibility of our promises.

Kiritsis barricaded himself in his apartment and warned the police that he had wired the walls and entrances so that the dynamite he claimed to have would detonate if anyone attempted a forced entry. Although the trained dogs had not "hit" on any dynamite, Kiritsis' background made his threat highly plausible. As was later discovered, what he had rigged up was merely a lighted candle hung by string over some open gasoline containers. The 25 sticks of dynamite Kiritsis had acquired were later found in his car.

By the time Kiritsis had reached his apartment with his hostage, the Indianapolis police were already surrounding the building. More than 500 residents were evacuated from the immediate area, and some 200 police dug in for what one officer predicted would be a long siege. Predictions of this sort, whether true or not, are probably tactically sound in such situations. They serve to allay the expectations that some quick resolution of the problem may be forthcoming. Since time provides the best single strategical weapon, such predictions establish an atmosphere conducive to the calm, unhurriedness which we know to be effective. If the authorities either explicitly or by implication indicate that they intend or expect to achieve a quick solution, the atmosphere at the scene can become dangerously charged with emotion. All of the participants may be infected by the expectation that something is going to happen momentarily. Such expectation can act as a self-fulfilling prophecy; i.e., the behavior of those involved makes it more likely that something will, in fact, happen momentarily. Unhappily, that something is almost certain to be dangerous or at least counterproductive to an effective solution of the problem. We know that people do act in ways which tend to make their own predictions of the outcomes of any event more likely. It is this sort of self-fulfilling prophecy which often characterizes the losers of the world. Expecting to fail they may quite unconsciously act in ways which make such failure more probably than had they not expected to fail. It is as if they can at least have the perverse satisfaction of knowing that their predictions were correct.

All of us are prone to such behavior. Thus it is far better to establish a public prediction that such hostage situations will take a long time to resolve successfully so that all concerned both consciously and unconsciously act in ways which are conducive to allowing time to have its significant effects. It is in this sense that one can almost say that, in a sense, doing nothing in such situations may be our most aggressive weapon. Or at least doing nothing which assumes that these incidents can be resolved quickly. Patience is not just a virtue in these situations, it is a crucial strategic weapon. During the Cotton incident, for example, every time some official asked how things were going, my response was to look at my watch and say, "Well, the hostages have now been alive for another hour. It must be going all right."

At the point in my lectures when I have tried to argue to my skeptical police students, the merits of doing nothing, I usually comment that although it is practically impossible, there is nothing **theoretically** wrong with considering walking away from a barricade or hostage situation. The reaction I get is explosive. Police are action-oriented, they are used to making rapid, life and death decisions. To even suggest that we might consider doing nothing is tantamount to advocating dereliction of duty. Clearly, that is not what I am saying. Instead, it is our expectations and attitudes toward such incidents which the possibility of inaction is intended to emphasize. Nonetheless, at one such lecture, a young officer from a small, rural force tentatively raised his hand to announce that he had, in fact, walked away from such a situation. With some trepidation regarding the reactions of his classmates he went on to relate the following incident:

While on patrol in a single, he was dispatched on a family quarrel signal. When he arrived at the house of the disputants, he was warned by the husband that if he attempted to enter the house, the husband would kill him and the wife. The responding officer at this point simply said, "OK, I'm leaving," and did just that! After re-entering his patrol car and driving just far enough away so that he could not be observed, the officer sat and waited. About an hour later the husband emerged from the house, unarmed, and the officer promptly arrested him. Dumbfounded, I asked the officer how in the world he could have thought he could avoid the severe disciplinary action such a response certainly would have produced. His reply was simple. He laughed briefly and said the Chief had been out of town. Before we return to the Kiritsis story, it is equally important to point out that some forms of decisive action may serve the same purposes as inaction.

While on assignment with the special task force of the New York State Police, I had the following experience. For a period just short of a week, our detail working bomb security at the Plattsburg campus hosting the American Olympic Team in the summer of 1976, had been suffering all of the effects of the boring routine of nothing happening. You will recall that expectations of terrorist activity centering around the Bicentennial celebration, and particularly the Olympic Games, had produced a state of police readiness until then unequaled in scope and manpower. Nothing, it seems to me, is more difficult to handle than the conflicting emotions involved in staying at a high pitch of readiness in the face of the boredom of nothing happening. Even the bomb dogs looked bored despite the constant simulations and searches. The command trailer was constantly filled with men milling about almost hoping that at least something would happen.

Sometime late in the afternoon on one of those hot, boring summer days, it did happen. The command trailer was galvanized by an APB put out by the Plattsburg Police Department reporting that "an unstable" suspect had kidnapped at gun point his teenage daughter, her girlfriend and another male youth in two separate armed forays into the boy's house and the girlfriend's house. The report indicated that the suspect had driven off and his whereabouts were unknown. A subsequent information bulletin indicated that the suspect, now identified as an employee of the local penitentiary, had been heard to say that he "was going to teach the kids a lesson." No further amplification of the original report that he was "unstable" was forthcoming.

The squad to which I was attached, under the direction of T/Sgt. W. Hornberger not only handles bomb disposal but is also responsible for and equipped to handle hostage problems. Although clearly not related to the Olympic athletes we were assigned to guard, this was a problem tailor-made for our team. Everyone immediately donned his "second-chance" and raced for the waiting cars. While enroute to the Plattsburg Police Department offices to offer our help, another bulletin reporting gunshots was broadcast. By the time we had checked in with the Plattsburg command and started out to the reported location of the gunfire, we learned that one of the area state police officers already had the suspect in custody and was enroute to the state police barracks. The report indicated that the suspect arrested was the same man wanted in connection with the alleged kidnappings. In less than 30 minutes from the time of the original report, the suspect had been located and apprehended.

We proceeded to the troop barracks and talked with the arresting officer, a thirty-year veteran of the force. We learned that he had responded to the gunfire report to find the suspect, his back turned, standing before three teenage youths some 15 yards just off a back road. The officer told us that he had pulled up beside the suspect, gotten out of his car and had approached the suspect without unholstering his weapon. As the suspect turned to face him, the officer observed the weapon and said something to the effect of, "What the hell's going on here, give me that goddamn gun," and the suspect immediately handed over the weapon. Problem solved.

This thirty-year man, a tough, experienced sergeant, at first reacted to our questions with some puzzlement. It was quite clear that he thought the whole thing rather routine. As we continued to talk with him, however, it became clear that he was beginning to wonder if it had after all been so routine. I asked whether he had heard the report on the "unstable" kidnapping suspect and whether he had thought that this gunfire call might have involved the same person, particularly after he had spotted the "hostages." He indicated that he had thought so. I asked why he hadn't radioed back for help, established a perimeter and awaited additional units. He shrugged and indicated that, as was obvious, he hadn't needed any help and, as we all admitted, he was perfectly right. We congradulated him and left.

To this day I wonder what might have happened. Suppose the sergeant had pulled up far short of the suspect as soon as he had observed him and had radioed back for assistance? We were already enroute and would have arrived within minutes. We would have undoubtedly established a perimeter, assigned the rifle men to protected positions and instituted all the procedures of a potential hostage negotiation. I wonder if we would have thought in those first few minutes to ask the suspect to give up. It is possible that in our concern to follow procedures, we may not have gotten around to the obvious for quite some time. The obvious being to simply tell the suspect to give up. The sergeant, at considerable personal risk, had prevented a hostage situation which **we could have produced**. No one could possibly expect or advise anyone to place himself in such personal danger, but the lesson is nonetheless clear: we must not become so concerned with playing it by the book that we fail to take the sort of decisive action which may resolve the problem. At the very least, we must remember to periodically ask the suspect to give up!

We are all involved in the disconcerting paradox of trying to be ready for situations which our preparation is designed to prevent from happening. If we forget that our ultimate goal is to end the hostage incident without loss of life or injury, and instead make the procedures for dealing with such incidents our goal, we risk unnecessarily extending such incidents or even potentially producing what we are trying to prevent. Thus, there are two extremes: (1) doing nothing and, (2) taking dangerously precipitative action. Each of the two incidents exemplifying these two extremes ended well. Nothing quite succeeds like success. Neither extreme, however, has much to recommend it; they are dangerous solutions which cannot be expected to often end in success. The two incidents do indicate, however, that at least two ingredients can be expected to be effective. If doing nothing at all can, at least in some instances, be effective, then patience certainly can be effective. If taking decisive action worked for our state police sergeant, then authoritative demeanor can be expected to be useful in such situations. Together they produce what every textbook describes as the "quiet authority" advised for dealing with emotional crises.

No one expected Anthony Kiritsis to simply give up. By his declaration, he intended to hold his hostage until his demands were met. Kiritsis wanted complete immunity from prosecution or psychiatric treatment, cancellation of his $130,000 mortgage debt and a public apology from the mortgage company for the wrongs done him. Superficially, these demands would appear to be instrumental in character. That is to say, if one could believe that any assurances of immunity from prosecution would be valid under such conditions, what Kiritsis demanded would have achieved the solution to his problem, and was at least **thinkably** possible. Unlike other hostage-takers, Kiritsis was not asking for the freeing of all "political" prisoners, the feeding of all of the poor or the abdication of the American government. But it is difficult to see how any sane person could really believe that these demands would be met, and that even if met would be valid after surrender. Thus, Kiritsis' behavior either must be interpreted as expressive or simply insane.

Insanity implies that Kiritsis' behavior should have been disorganized and senseless. There can be no doubt that his behavior was not exemplary of what most would consider rational, but none of those present were prepared to conclude that Kiritsis was actively psychotic. What is left is the conclusion that his acts were designed to humiliate and terrorize his victim. If he could accomplish that expressive goal and remain immune from prosecution, so much the better. But, it would be my interpretation that the instrumental goals were distinctly secondary to the expressive ones. Thus, while holding the authorities at bay and negotiating the terms of his instrumental demands, Kiritsis was succeeding at his expressive display. In such situations, there is little that can be negotiated with respect to the expressive component except to provide the sort of climate which allows it to run its course in such a fashion as to prevent harm to the victim. More positive steps can, however, be taken with respect to the instrumental goals of the perpetrator. By emphasizing these instrumental aspects, the negotiations can focus on the rational components of the situation, and thus, by exclusion, diminish the more volatile and dangerous emotive aspects.

Twelve hours into the siege, the board chairman of the real estate and mortgage companies involved went before the television cameras to offer Kiritsis a public apology. The chairman declared that the companies had influenced two grocery stores and a restaurant not to locate on the property owned by Kiritsis and offered him damage payment for "the wrong we may have caused Mr. Kiritsis." Public vindication of these kinds of perpetrators has become virtually routine. The Croatian skyjackers demanded and received newspaper space for the publication of their long and rambling manifesto. In addition, they demanded and received air drops of leaflets over New York City, publicizing their cause. There is hardly an incident which does not give media time to the angry denunciations of the perpetrator or the abject pleas of the victims. The public's identification with the problems of such perpetrators disposes them to believe that the perpetrators are justified in their actions. We have always been rather unreasonably predisposed toward the underdog, even when his behavior is destructive and criminal. The media involvement in such incidents finally culminated in the establishment of guidelines adopted by the industry after the nearly disasterous events of the Hanafi actions in Washington.* It is difficult to overstate the effect which this sort of media exposure can have on other perpetrators and upon our own national character.

Suppose it is indeed true that the mortgage company had wrongfully prevented the development of the Kiritsis property so that they might foreclose on it. What effect does such a public admission have upon the conclusions to be drawn by the viewers? It seems clear that no matter what its effect upon Kiritsis, any such gain must be weighed against the deleterious effect of achieving such admission at gun point. Suppose the admission was false? Then, it seems to me, we have publicly displayed our willingness to use any subterfuge or deceit to effect the successful resolution of the problem. Such expediency seems to me to be contradictory to the principles of justness our resolution of the problem is designed to maintain. Where the means are clearly antithetical to their ends, I cannot see how they may be justified by that end.

By the end of the second day of the siege, the last of Kiritsis' demands was given public compliance. Wednesday night, Prosecutor James A. Kelly authorized an offer of immunity which included no arrest and no psychiatric commitment if Kiritsis would release his hostage. Kiritsis demanded that independent legal opinions of the validity of this immunity pledge be obtained, and declared that he "would sleep on" the offer. His earlier reaction to the public apology from the board chairman had been that he was still dissatisfied and that it was "not adequate." Frankly, with the assurance of hindsight and ignorance, I am not at all surprised. To the outside observer it

---

*See the material in Chapter four.

appeared that we were ready to, and indeed did, comply with all of his demands. These concessions, and the public vindication of the justification of his actions in seeking them must have enormously puffed-up Kiritsis. In fact, when Kiritsis finally surrendered Thursday evening, he declared, "Get the cameras on. Get those cameras on. I'm a god-damned national hero and don't forget it." With the shotgun still strapped to his victim's neck, he delivered a half-hour cursing oration before the live television cameras before finally releasing his hostage. In a swaggering gesture, Kiritsis then fired the shotgun out of the window with the declaration that "I've wanted to fire this thing ever since I've had it." At this point, he was immediately surrounded by police and handcuffed. Kiritsis' reaction can only be described as one of astonished surprise. Police Chief Eugene Gallagher explained to him: "Tony, you lied. You said you would let that man go before you came down." After Kiritsis was safely in jail, the local authorities went before the television cameras to carefully explain that they had never had any intention of keeping their promises of immunity, that they had lied deliberately in order to secure Kiritsis' surrender and the safe release of his hostage. This dramatic admission carried coast to coast undoubtedly will significantly affect all hostage negotiations to come.

This precedent-setting incident has one final wrinkle which should be discussed. Contrary to our recommendations not to bring family members to the scene, and to most other guidelines for such situations, the brother of Kiritsis was brought to talk with him. In a brief conversation through the slightly open door, Kiritsis is reported to have said to his brother, "I love you. I don't want to hurt anybody and I don't want to go to jail." In the estimation of those witnessing the exchange, this brief interview was a significant turning point in the negotiations. Although Kiritsis did not immediately surrender or relent in his demands, apparently the tone of the negotiations became more subdued and less vitriolic. At one point later on, Kiritsis declared that the police "are lucky they're dealing with me and I'm stable." The brother was not apparently in any danger of himself becoming a hostage or of becoming an untrained and complicating principal in the negotiating efforts, the two primary reasons usually given as contra-indications for such a tactic. Unlike here, however, there have been instances in which civilians have produced unmanageable and dangerous complications.

The Kiritsis case has been included in this book as an illustration of several important themes relevant to hostage negotiation: the need for patience and deliberation balanced with **appropriate** levels of action; problems associated with promises made, whether for immunity or other outcomes; the expressive versus instrumental goals of the perpetrator; and possible complications when perpetrator relatives become involved.

Anthony Kiritsis was tried and found "not guilty by reason of insanity."

4 / The Hanafi Muslim Case

On Wednesday, March 9, 1977, shortly after 11:00 A.M., our nation's capital city was invaded. In a combined attack, 12 terrorists of the Hanafi Muslim sect led by Hamaas Khaalis occupied three separate locations and held more than 100 hostages in a siege that was to last some 40 hours. Khaalis and six others began their attack by occupying the headquarters of B'nai B'rith, the Jewish service organization. Dressed in jeans, with long knives strapped to their hips, they burst into the lobby of the building carrying an assortment of rifles, swords, shotguns and even a crossbow. When Wesley Hymes tried to escape, one of the raiders slashed his hand with the machete he was carrying, and then shot him in the arm. Khaalis shouted at the startled occupants of the lobby, "They killed my babies and shot my women. Now they will listen to us or heads will roll."

Before he became the avenging warrior of his Muslim cause, Hamaas Khaalis had been Ernest Timothy McGhee of Gary, Indiana. A former jazz musician and war-on-poverty worker with a bachelor's degree in social science, the 56-year-old Khaalis had a long record of psychiatric commitments and apparent mental instability. In 1973, at the time Khaalis had become the leader of the factional sect of the American Black Muslim movement known as the Hanafi, a group of rival Black Muslims raided the group's headquarters in Washington. Upon his return to the mansion, Khaalis found his 10-day-old son drowned in a sink, two of his other children and his grandchild drowned in a bathtub, and his remaining two children shot to death. Two adults who had been in the house at the time had also been slain. Five Black Muslim sect members were subsequently apprehended, convicted and given life sentences for the murders before the year was to end. But Khaalis remained unsatisfied. He seethed in rage over the lack of true retribution dictated by his beloved *Koran* and his feeling that the Black Muslim leaders had not been sufficiently punished.

Khaalis and other strict followers of the Islamic teachings considered the Chicago-based movement of Black Muslims to be blasphemous heretics to the true faith. The Black Muslims, according to these believers, had fatally departed from orthodoxy in accepting W. D. Fard, an itinerant peddler, as God and naming Elijah Poole, later known as Elijah Muhammad, as Fard's prophet. After his discharge from the army, McGhee had converted to the Moslem faith and taken the religious name of Khaalis. He originally joined the Black Muslim movement in an attempt to steer them back to the orthodoxy he believed to be the true expression of Islam. Although he rose rapidly through the ranks and had worked closely with the powerful Malcolm X, Khaalis had little impact and left the movement in 1958 to found the Hanafi group. Largely composed of middle class blacks, he attracted to his ranks a number of influential athletes including basketball star Kareem Abdul-Jabbar who donated $78,000 to buy the Washington mansion housing the headquarters of the group. Just prior to the raid on these headquarters, Khaalis and his followers had written letters to the Black Muslim leaders denouncing their movement and their prophet. These denunciations were followed almost immediately by the raid and the murder of his family. This background made it clear that Khaalis' action on March ninth had all of the appearance of a holy war.

Khaalis and the six other raiders attacking the B'nai B'rith building moved quickly to the top floor and began rounding up hostages from the rest of the building. Moving through the building with trained and brutal precision, described by one of the hostages as "like Green Berets or something," they eventually secured more than 100 hostages within a defensive perimeter on the eighth floor. One of these hostages attempted to conceal the Star of David she wore around her neck and was butt-whipped by one of the gunmen for her efforts. Even before he had been assured that the building had been secured, Khaalis phoned back to his own headquarters and told his son-in-law, Abdul Aziz, "We're in," to which he received the reply, "Praise Allah!"

The first police response came as a result of the shouts and frantic gesticulations from the windows of those few who had escaped the roundup by barricading themselves in offices on the lower floors. At first the police assumed that they were dealing with ordinary gunmen possibly escaping from a bungled holdup. While they surrounded the building and deployed their S.W.A.T. teams, the Hanafi struck again. Three Hanafi raiders entered the Islamic Center carrying shotguns at 12:30 and demanded to speak to its director, Dr. Muhammad Rauf. The timing obviously prearranged by Khaalis, just as Rauf appeared, Khaalis telephoned the center from B'nai B'rith to tell Rauf that he was a traitor to Islam and that Rauf's native Egypt was trying to make peace with the Jews. The raiders then seized Rauf and 10 other visitors to the mosque.

Still the Hanafi group had not yet finished carrying out their attack plan. Shortly after 2 P.M., they launched their third attack on the District Building housing the offices of the Mayor of Washington. Two of the Hanafi, armed with a pistol and a shotgun, entered the building and took over an office on the fifth floor. Alerted by the elevator operator, a building security guard boarded the elevator to locate the gunmen. A second elevator carrying two young black reporters on their way to a routine meeting arrived on the fifth floor at the same time as the guard. Before anyone knew what was happening, one of the Hanafi raiders opened fire with his shotgun, wounding two of the men in the hallway and killing a third.

By this time, all of Washington was alerted. Although still uncertain as to whether the three raids represented a coordinated attack or who the perpetrators were, it was obvious to all that the authorities had a major calamity on their hands. President Carter, by now no stranger to the complications of such hostage incidents since his telephone role in the Corey Moore* episode on the very day of these Hanafi raids, ordered the FBI to mobilize its specially trained personnel to the scenes of the take-overs. At the State Department, Douglas Heck, special assistant to the Secretary of State in charge of terrorism research, conferred with his terrorist experts. Patrick J. Mullaney, one of the FBI's most experienced men in this field who had just assisted the Indianapolis police in the Kiritsis incident was ordered back to Washington from Cleveland where he had again successfully concluded negotiations with Corey Moore. At the least, the Hanafi were to be dealt with by what is probably the single greatest group of hostage experts to be found anywhere in the world. From this talent, negotiating teams were assembled at each of the attack sites.

By late afternoon, the nature of the Khaalis plan began to unfold. Max Robinson of WTOP-TV received a call from Abdul Aziz, Khaalis'

---

*On March 8, 1977, in Warrensville Heights, Ohio, Corey Moore took a local police captain hostage, and, as one of his demands in doing so, insisted that the President appear on television and apologize for "all the misdeeds done to blacks from the year 1619 to 1977."

son-in-law asking him to meet with Aziz. After explaining that it was his father-in-law whom Robinson had met after the massacre at the Hanafi headquarters, who was responsible for the attacks, Aziz had Robinson speak by phone with Khaalis. In a passionate diatribe, Khaalis outlined his demands. First, he wanted what he considered to be the blasphemous film, *Mohammed, Messenger of God,* premiering in New York and Los Angeles to be withdrawn. "We want the picture out of the country!" Khaalis declared. Second, he wanted the convicted participants in the raid on his headquarters brought to him along with the murderer of Malcolm X. Third, he wanted the police to reimburse him for the $750 fine levied against him for contempt of court incurred during the trial of the Black Muslims who had killed his children. Fourth, he wanted Secretary of State Vance and the ambassadors of all Moslem countries notified "because we are going to kill foreign Muslims at the Islamic Center and create an international incident."

Within hours of his takeover, Khaalis chose to release a number of the hostages from the B'nai B'rith location, and with them the first detailed reports of the hostages' treatment became available. Andrew Hoffman reported that they had asked him where his family was from. Although half Jewish, Hoffman told them his people came from Italy. Apparently satisfied, Khaalis escorted Hoffman to the stairs leading from their barricaded position and released him with the injunction to "get married and have lots of babies."

Later, others of the hostages, who were not so lucky, were to report a grimly frightening ordeal of taunting, constant threats of death by decapitation at the hands of their sword-brandishing captors, brutal beatings and anti-Semitic tirades. But, as we surely have come to expect in such situations, some found their captors not at all so bad. One B'nai B'rith secretary who had been appointed by Khaalis to answer the phones during the siege said of him afterwards, "He was very nice. He's basically a compassionate person." Khaalis and his men carefully separated the male and female hostages out of religious scruples. The women were treated far better than the male hostages. One of the women reported that "they made a fetish out of saying how they were not going to rape the women," and instructed all of them to cover their legs with newspapers complaining that by their Moslem standards they were indecently exposing themselves.

Khaalis was clearly the key to any hopes for a negotiated settlement. It was now clear that Khaalis was in command of the entire operation and that all three raids were part of the plan. At the other buildings, the other Hanafi raiders would not negotiate with the police and were in constant touch with Khaalis at the B'nai B'rith location. At the District Building, seven hostages were laid out on the floor of the fifth floor office, tied hand and foot, their captors wielding shotguns above them. In the Islamic Center, the hostages were allowed to sit in chairs and sat around drinking coffee and tea with their captors.

The first attempts to negotiate with Khaalis were arranged through Egypt's ambassador, Ashraf Ghorbal, who had already volunteered his services in the crisis. After enlisting the help of his fellow ambassador from Pakistan, Sahabzada Yaqub-Khan, who was also the acting director of the captured Islamic Center, the two men talked with Khaalis by phone. Yaqub-Khan recalled that Khaalis in that first conversation with him, "was in a very excitable mood. It was a very tense moment." Khaalis used the call to denounce the Moslem countries for not supporting his holy war against the Black Muslims and the other defilers of the faith. He complained that no one listened to him at the Islamic Center, and that he was a persecuted victim of his faith. The ambassadors considered that their task was, in the words of Ghorbal, "to establish rapport with Khaalis, to persuade him to release the hostages as a merciful action and to play to his religious sentiments to that end." This quote attributed to Ghorbol by *Newsweek* clearly sounds like the advice undoubtedly given to the ambassadors by the assembled experts. On that advice, Yaqub-Khan, with a specialist in the *Koran* beside him, began to read passages to Khaalis who retorted that he didn't need anyone to teach him the *Koran,* and that he knew the holy book of his faith better than the ambassador. Despite this unpromising beginning, it was clear that if the key to this siege was Khaalis, then the key to Khaalis was to be found in his dedication to his religion and his faith in the teachings of the *Koran.*

Joined by Iran's ambassador, Ardeshir Zahedi, who had arrived from Paris, the ambassadors again called Khaalis. Khaalis was told that the showing of the film was to be stopped, was given the $750 he had demanded and was implored to match these concessions by releasing the hostages. Two more phone calls were made during the early morning hours of that first day of the siege. In each, it appeared that little, if any, progress was being made except to allow Khaalis to ventilate his emotions. In the last of these phone calls, the Moslem ambassadors asked Khaalis to join them in the traditional morning prayer to Allah. Khaalis responded with angry vehemence to the suggestion, pointing out that the place he was in was filthy and unfit for prayer. He retorted with the observation that as Muslims the ambassadors should know better than to even make such a suggestion. According to those present at the time, his response was entirely consistent with Moslem tradition and confirmed Khaalis' knowledge of and dedication to his religion. Further, it indicated, in the opinion of one of the experts, what was probably a major influence in convincing Khaalis to leave the building — he reacted very negatively to the dirt and disarray with which he was surrounded. Later the authorities were to learn from the hostages that Khaalis insisted that the toilets be scrubbed before and after each use.

At one point, Khaalis was reminded of his promise to treat his prisoners well and asked to find out what food they wanted sent up to them. For something like two hours, Khaalis and his men acted as waiters, dutifully taking and relaying sandwich orders from each of the hostages. One hostage reported in amazement after his release that he had ordered an egg salad sandwich and actually had gotten just that. By this time, the negotiators elatedly observed a small but highly significant change in Khaalis. Although his angry denouncements and challenges did not abate, Khaalis subtly had changed from referring to his hostages as "captives" and "prisoners of war" to calling them simply "people." This humanization of his victims from abstract, symbolic targets of his grievances to persons who could be hungry, frightened and uncomfortable was the first glimmer of hope that the end was in sight.

Deputy Chief Rabe, his performance described by all as extraordinarily expert during the siege, acted as the principal police contact with Khaalis. Throughout the first night and the next day, the eighth floor phone of B'nai B'rith was nearly constantly ringing with calls from all sorts of people. Although Khaalis refused to talk with many of these callers, some did get through and considerably complicated the attempts to negotiate with him. In addition to those who called to read passages from the *Koran* to Khaalis or even to offer to exchange themselves as hostages, the news media added their own disruptive influence during these critical first hours of negotiation. The following excerpts from three separate interviews as reported by the *New York Times* exemplify the character of these conversations.

WMAL Interview

Khaalis: We came in to fight to the death. And there'll be a lot of good people won't come out, either — you know that.

Q. You are said to want the five men convicted of the killings (of Hanafi sect people in Washington) brought to you. Correct?

A. That's right. They were laughing in court, jesting and making fun. The Cassius Clay gang was laughing when we were bringing out the biers of our little babies and children. (The small

Hanafi sect has a running vendetta with the bigger Black Muslim sect, of which the world heavyweight boxing champion Muhammad Ali, formerly known as Cassius Clay, is a member.)

Q. Do you expect the demand to be fulfilled?

A. That's up to the Government. If they don't, the worst is to come.

Q. What do you have in mind?

A. They can sit along and watch my family all day long for the next two years. If it won't be from here, it will be from somewhere else where you least expect. It will be worse.

(Mr. Khaalis was asked if progress was made in his overnight phone contacts with government officials:)

A. That's up to the Government. If they play games, it would be very bad . . . very, very bad; very, very grave. If they try any funny business, very grave. If we are all killed, it would be worse next time. Some other place. There's nothing nobody can do about it.

WBBM-TV Interview

Khaalis: I want those that walked into my house. I want them! Are you listening? It has not even begun. We've been nice so far. We have some more wild men out there, in the name of Allah, for their faith — wild in the way of faith, because they believe it to the death. You just tell Cassius Clay and Wallace X and Herbert that they got to report here to Washington, D.C., because people's lives depend upon it.

Q. You want them too . . .?

A. I want them to come here. They're not big people. They're roaches and rats and gangsters. I want them here. I want the killers here!

Q. Well, we're all very worried about it, Sir.

A. Well, you — you — well, then you get on the phone and call President Carter and some of those senators that never even sent a call, a condolence message. Do you realize when my family was wiped out, not one said one word? Not one. Not even a preacher. Not even a minister. Not even a spiritual advisor. Not even a City Council member. So, I'm very glad you're worried now. Huh? When they wiped out my family, I didn't hear about your sympathy and emotions. I got a letter the other day from my brother telling me how the brother was swaggering around in jail, the killer of Malcolm, walking around with guards protecting him. Well, tell him it's over. Tell him it's payday.

Q. But why is today payday?

A. Why? Why? Payday always comes. Don't you know you have a payday coming? We all have to report.

Q. You're not going to hurt anyone, are you?

A. I'm a soldier. What do soldiers do? They protect and they defend. And I have a wife and children that were taken out for nothing by killers.

Q. But these people you have had nothing to do with it.

A. All right, but I'm a soldier. So, they same way when this army marches into countries. Right? There're people that have — don't have a lot of things to do nothing with it. Right? Come on, now. Back up, now. Stop all this piety. Let's tell the truth. Stop it all. How many civilians do have anything to do with it when war comes? Don't they pay the higher price? Come on now, we're at war.

AP Interview

Q. Are you making any progress in your negotiations?

A. That's up to the Government. The Government can play if it wants to, and it's going to find out. You can see one side of the moon, right? The other you don't, right? O.K. That answers that.

Q. How about the other demands, about the. . . . ?

A. Well, that's up to the Government. You see, they got a lot to cry over tomorrow, too, haven't they, if they've been playing games?

Q. Have you set any deadlines?

A. I say they have a lot to be crying over, don't they? No, we're not going to set deadlines. This way, they're going to find out that I'm not joking. They can play if they want to, and this way they can find out that I'm not joking. No, uh-uh. I'm not like that. I know that they don't hold fast to their promises. You know, like the man out there in Indiana? Hey, remember? No, they don't hold fast to their promises, and then they brag about it. See, all they did was made it worse. You understand? We know that, already. When we walked in here.

Q. Well, then, what are you waiting for?

A. Don't you worry about it. I know what I'm doing.

Q. You're the leader.

A. Allah let me be the leader. Even wild horses have a leader, so there's nothing wrong with that. Don't call us no Black Muslims.

Q. No, I won't do that.

A. I'll beat the hell out of somebody over here. You'll cause somebody to get a head beating. You're not listening, see? The Zionist press wants to keep twisting things. And we're not gonna have it that way. They try to tell the people Cassius and Wallace are Moslems. We going to stop this foolishness. Everybody's going to know.

Q. We're not referring to you, we haven't been referring to you as Black Muslims.

A. Don't put that stigma on us. We don't call people by those South African terms.

From these interviews, Khaalis learned that Wallace Muhammad, the leader of the Black Muslims, was at that moment at the Washington Airport. This knowledge and the reporters' prodding about the demands as yet unsatisfied only served to inflame Khaalis. The negotiator's delaying tactics and attempt to avoid discussion of Khaalis' demands to have those whom he considered responsible for the deaths of his children brought to him were suddenly and frustratingly defeated by the news that one of his principal enemies was, in fact, already in Washington.

Another critical moment came on Thursday when it was learned that there would be the traditional 19 cannon salute to the visiting British Ambassador. Fearful that the noise might be mistaken by Khaalis as an assault on him or his comrades in the other locations, the ceremony was quickly cancelled.

Late Thursday, Khaalis called to ask for a face-to-face meeting with Ambassador Yaqub-Khan. When Washington police chief, Cullinane, and his deputy chief, Rabe, suggested that Khaalis come out into the street unarmed, Khaalis vehemently refused. He instead demanded that the ambassador come to him. Yaqub-Khan's colleagues thought that he would be in too great danger if he were to enter alone and offered the compromise of meeting Khaalis in the lobby of the building along with Cullinane, Rabe, Captain J. O'Brien of the metropolitan force, all three ambassadors and Khaalis' son-in-law, Abdul Aziz. Khaalis agreed.

Grandly entering the lobby, Khaalis greeted the ambassadors in Arabic and exchanged embraces with them. After some three hours of discussion, Khaalis finally responded to the pleas that at least some of the hostages be freed as "a gesture of good faith" by offering all of the hostages, provided he was allowed to be free pending his trial, which he both expected and accepted. Khaalis was not asking for immunity as had Kiritsis, but he argued that he would lose face with his followers if he were to surrender and be taken into custody. District law did, in fact, allow for self-recognizance release in lieu of bail under judicial discretion. Attorney General Bell was contacted for a determination of whether or not the negotiators could comply with Khaalis' demand. Bell and others are reported to have been troubled by the precedent such an action would create. After all, Khaalis bore the direct responsibility of the death at the hands of his cohorts of one man at the District Building and the wounding of at least three others. Despite the fact that Khaalis was furious with his men over this unnecessary carnage, it was clear that his misgivings in no way mitigated his culpability. Nonetheless, with the assurance that this concession would finally end the siege, Washington Superior Court Judge Harold Greene agreed to release Khaalis without bail pending his arraignment and trial. By 5 A.M., Friday, some 40 hours after it had begun, the siege finally ended.

This incident probably represents some sort of high-water mark of the recent scourge of hostage crises in the United States. Like the skyjackings which preceded these most recent outbreaks, these manifestations seem to run a common course. Each successive incident is followed by a furor of publicity pandering to the public interest until finally both the media and they are sated by one last incident which in scope and drama surfeits their desires. Skyjacking ended not so much because we better guarded our airports, but because the public became sufficiently bored and frightened by the crime to insist upon better security. The Hanafi incident finally spurred the national news media to take a long hard look at their possible influence on such events. On April 7, the Director of CBS News, Richard Salant, issued a set of guidelines for the coverage of such incidents. These guidelines, made part of the "CBS News Standards" read as follows:

Coverage of Terrorists

Because the facts and circumstances of each case vary, there can be no specific self-executing rules for the handling of terrorist/hostage stories. CBS News will continue to apply the normal tests of news judgment and if, as so often they are, these stories are newsworthy, we must continue to give them coverage despite the dangers of "contagion." The disadvantages of suppression are, among other things, (1) adversely affecting our credibility ("What else are the news people keeping from us?");

(2) giving free rein to sensationalized and erroneous word-of-mouth rumors; (3) distorting our news judgments for some extraneous judgmental purpose. These disadvantages compel us to continue to provide coverage. Nevertheless in providing for such coverage, there must be thoughtful, conscientious care and restraint. Obviously, the story should not be sensationalized beyond the actual fact of its being sensational. We should exercise particular care in how we treat the terrorist/kidnapper. More specifically:

1. An essential component of the story is the demands of the terrorist/kidnapper and we must report those demands. But we should avoid providing an excessive platform for the terrorist/kidnapper. Thus, unless such demands are succinctly stated and free of rhetoric and propaganda, it may be better to paraphrase the demands instead of presenting them directly through the voice or picture of the terrorist/kidnapper.

2. Except in the most compelling circumstances, and then only with the approval of the President of CBS News, or in his absence, the Senior Vice-President of News, there should be no live coverage of the terrorist/kidnapper, since we may fall into the trap of providing an unedited platform for him. (This does **not** limit live on-the-spot reporting by CBS News reporters, but care should be exercised to assure restraint and context.)

3. News personnel should be mindful of the probable need by the authorities who are dealing with the terrorist for communication by telephone and hence should endeavor to ascertain, wherever feasible, whether our own use of such lines would be likely to interfere with the authorities' communications.

4. Responsible CBS News representatives should endeavor to contact experts dealing with the hostage situation to determine whether they have any guidance on such questions as phraseology to be avoided, what kinds of questions or reports might tend to exacerbate the situation, etc. Any such recommendations by established authorities on the scene should be carefully considered as guidance (but not as instruction) by CBS News personnel.

5. Local authorities should also be given the name or names of CBS personnel whom they can contact should they have further guidance or wish to deal with such delicate questions as a newsman's call to the terrorists or other matters which

might interfere with authorities dealing with the terrorists.

6. Guidelines affecting our coverage of civil disturbances are also applicable here, especially those which relate to avoiding the use of inflammatory catchwords or phrases, the reporting of rumors, etc. As in the case of policy dealing with civil disturbances, in dealing with a hostage story, reporters should obey all police instructions but report immediately to their superiors any such instructions that seem to be intended to manage or suppress the news.

7. Coverage of this kind of story should be in such overall balance as to length that it does not unduly crowd out other important news of the hour/day.

There is much to applaud in Mr. Salant's attempt to wrestle with the dilemmas faced by a free and responsible press. But, I would differ with at least one critical and major point in these guidelines. It seems to me that there is, in fact, more danger of bias in coverage when the media **prohibit** reporting the exact and rhetoric-laden demands of a perpetrator. It is the intemperateness, the unreasonableness, the irrationality of these perpetrators which we must come to understand and know. If we had not seen Kiritsis' angry, childlike display of swaggering braggadocio, he might well have been remembered as the "hero" he thought himself to be. If the "rhetoric" of Khaalis had not been heard by millions, they might have thought him reasonably justified in his sought-for vengeance against the killers of his children.

These perpetrators are their own worst representatives. If they have the advantage of a temperate, rational mouthpiece through which to express their irrationality, they gain rather than lose. I firmly believe that there is more to be gained in giving these disturbed, often pathological, criminals direct exposure to our scrutiny. That exposure can effectively act to allay our natural impulses toward identifying with those who feel they have been oppressed or wronged. It is difficult to sympathize or identify with the ranting irrationality of Khaalis' choice of rhetoric no matter how moved we may be by the brutal murder of his children. The picture of Kiritsis brutally debasing his victim after he had seemingly won all of the concessions he had demanded, could not fail to outrage even those prepared to believe the worst of his realtor captive.

To have "paraphrased" the demands of the SLA would have meant to have made them eminently reasonable. Who among CBS's viewers could not have agreed that the poor and oppressed of the world should be helped and fed? Without their "platforms" these criminals would rise in stature. The universal forms of expression of their demands are themselves the transparent denial of all that is either just or rational. If we expurgate the "mother f-----, pig, facist insect" rhetoric surrounding the "platforms" of our Cinques, we make them better and thus only less real. I frankly cannot conceive of CBS News "paraphrasing" Hamaas Khaalis' anti-Semitic diatribes. Even to put such vile garbage in the third person would be so tasteless that they would surely avoid it as giving "an excessive platform" to Khaalis and his racist followers. But from the mouth of Khaalis, it is direct and accurate reporting. It needs no interpretation.

The Hanafi Muslim incident, and the manner in which it was resolved, has much to teach us. It highlights the special problems of coordination, personnel and negotiations which occur when the hostage event involves multiple perpetrators, many hostages and more than one hostage site. It is a good example of the careful and coordinated use of both highly skilled police personnel and non-police, but highly relevant, authorities of other types. It underscores how crucial to the outcome can be our efforts to understand the perpetrators' motivations. And it raises, as have most hostage events, important and still-not-resolved questions about media responsibility and about the legal and social consequences of promises made in an effort to secure release of hostages.

5 / The Hearst Case

On February 4, 1974 Patricia Randolph Hearst was kidnapped from her Berkeley apartment where she was living with Steven Weed. From that date until nineteen-and-a-half months later when she was finally apprehended (or "released"), no single kidnapping, including that of the Lindberg case, has attracted more widespread publicity and interest. There is hardly a single corner of the world which is unaware of the details of this sensational case. From only a few days after her kidnapping until June 7, 1974, seven tapes were made and delivered to the public by the SLA and their victim. Made a part of the SLA's conditions for the safe return of Patricia Hearst, these tapes relaying their demands, remonstrations, rationalizations and protestations were to be broadcast to the world at large.

THE CAST OF CHARACTERS

Donald DeFreeze (30), a.k.a. Cinque, Field Marshal of the SLA.

Born to a lower class black family in a Cleveland ghetto, engaged in street crime at an early age, he was frequently arrested for petty crimes and possession of guns, and was sentenced to California prisons for holdup attempts in Los Angeles. In prison, he took the name Cinque, after the leader of the 1839 slave revolt on the slave ship *Amistad*. Cinque escaped Soledad Prison and founded the SLA with Patricia Soltysik (a.k.a. Zoya) in the summer of 1973. He died in a shootout with the police. According to the coroner's report, the immediate cause of

This chapter originally appeared under the title: "Psycholinguistic Analysis of the Symbionese Liberation Army" in *Assets Protection*, Vol. 1, No. 4, 1976 death was a point-blank gunshot wound to the temple, suggesting a suicide.

Patricia Hearst (21) a.k.a. Tania, kidnap victim of the SLA who became a member of the SLA.

Born the third of five daughters to the wealthy Hearst family of California, she attended private schools and was not known to engage in politics. At the University of California at Berkeley, she was an art history major. At the time of her kidnapping (February 4, 1974), she was living with her fiancé, Steven Weed. During the time of her captivity, she assumed the name Tania (companion to Ché Guevara in the Bolivian Revolution). On September 18, 1975 she was captured by the FBI in San Francisco and subsequently convicted on two counts of a federal indictment for bank robbery.

William Harris (30), a.k.a. Teko, a general in the SLA.

Born to a white middle class family in Carmel, Indiana. After graduating high school, he served with the Marines for eight months in Vietnam. He joined the 1967 march on the Pentagon and took part in demonstrations at the 1968 Democratic National Convention. Harris graduated from Indiana University with a master's degree in theater. While at the University, he met and married Emily Schwartz (Yolanda). After moving to Oakland, California, Teko and his wife, Yolanda, became involved with Venceremos, the now-defunct Maoist group. Teko, Yolanda and Patricia managed to avoid capture by authorities for several months after a shoot-out which killed six SLA members, but all were captured by the FBI on the same day in September 1975.

Angela Atwood (25), a.k.a. Gelina, a general in the SLA.

Born to a white lower middle class family in Paterson, New Jersey. At Indiana University she studied acting and became friends of William and Emily Harris. After an unsuccessful marriage and deep involvement in the Women's Movement, Gelina began an affair with Joseph Remiro, an SLA soldier who was convicted in the murder of an Oakland school superintendent. Gelina was also active in Bay area prison work. She died in the SLA shoot-out with police.

Nancy Ling Perry (26), a.k.a. Fahizah (i.e., "one who is victorious"), a soldier in the SLA.

Born to a white middle class family in Santa Rosa, California. In her high school years she was known as a cheerleader and Barry Goldwater supporter. She attended the University of California at Berkeley, majoring in English. She is reported to have been a heavy drug user. In 1967 she married a black musician, Gilbert Perry, but the marriage ended within a short time. She went on to work as a topless dancer. Fahizah became romantically involved with Russell Little, a prison-reform activist who was later convicted with Joseph Remiro in the murder of the Oakland school superintendent. It was Fahizah who wrote an open letter claiming SLA credit for the Oakland killing, labeling the superintendent as a repressive figure in the school system. She died in the shoot-out with the police.

Emily Harris (28), a.k.a. Yolanda, a soldier in the SLA.

Born to a white upper class family in the suburb of Clarendon Hall, outside of Chicago. She was known for her straight-A performance in school. While studying for a degree in English at Indiana University, she met and married William Harris. Emily became deeply involved in the Women's Movement and prison reform. She was captured by the FBI in San Francisco.

CHRONOLOGY OF MAJOR EVENTS IN THE HEARST CASE

November 6, 1973

Marcus Foster, a black school administrator in Oakland is shot dead. The SLA claims responsibility for the killing. SLA soldiers Joseph Remiro and Russell Little are later convicted for the murder of Foster.

February 4, 1974

Patricia Hearst is kidnapped from her apartment in Berkeley by two men and one woman. Steven Weed, Miss Hearst's fiancé, is left beaten in the apartment.

February 7, 1974

The SLA sends letter to Berkeley radio station KPFA claiming responsibility for the kidnapping.

February 8, 1974

The SLA releases tape recording #1, in which they demand that Randolph A. Hearst, Patricia's father, provide a food program for the needy in California.

February 16, 1974

The SLA releases tape #2. On the tape, Patricia attempts to clear up confusion over the SLA requirements for the food distribution.

February 18, 1974

Randolph Hearst announces that he will pledge two million dollars for the food program.

February 19, 1974

The SLA releases tape #3, demanding four million dollars more in food ransom.

March 3, 1974

Mr. and Mrs. Hearst plead for some message from Patricia.

March 9, 1974

Tape #4 is released. On the tape Patricia accuses her parents of inaction. The SLA demands higher quality food and national broadcast time for two jailed SLA members, Joseph Remiro and Russell Little. Californians begin receiving food from the Hearst program.

March 11, 1974

Randolph Hearst promises he will attempt to meet the demands of the SLA for more food.

April 2, 1974

The SLA sends message indicating their intentions to release Patricia. Randolph Hearst and the Hearst Corporation put four million dollars in escrow, which is to be spent for food upon the safe release of Miss Hearst.

April 3, 1974

Tape #5 is released. Patricia states that she has decided to join the SLA rather than be released.

April 15, 1974

The SLA robs the Hibernia Bank in San Francisco and shoots two bystanders. Miss Hearst is identified as one of the five persons participating in the holdup. Miss Hearst, initially sought by the FBI as a material witness, is now charged with robbery.

April 24, 1974

The SLA releases tape #6. Members of the SLA give an explanation of the robbery. Patricia refers to herself as "Tania," strongly denounces her family and states she was a willing participant in the bank robbery.

May 3, 1974

The deadline set by Randolph Hearst and the Hearst Corporation for release of Patricia expires, and four million dollars is withdrawn from escrow.

May 16, 1974

William Harris (Teko) is accused of shoplifting in an Inglewood, California sporting goods store. Patricia aids Harris's escape by firing a machine gun at the store. William Harris, Emily Harris (Yolanda) and Patricia are reported to have stolen a number of cars to evade police and allegedly taken captive 19-year-old Thomas Matthews for several hours.

May 17, 1974

Six SLA members are killed in a shoot-out with the police at their hideout in Los Angeles. The SLA dead are: Donald DeFreeze, Nancy Ling Perry, Patricia Soltysik, William Wolfe, Camilla Hall and Angela Atwood.

May 22, 1974

Patricia is charged with a number of criminal acts and placed on the most-wanted list.

May 23, 1974

Coroner makes determination that Donald DeFreeze (Cinque) committed suicide during the May 17th shoot-out.

June 7, 1974

Tape #7 is released. Teko, Yolanda and Tania give eulogies for the dead SLA members. Patricia tells of her love for SLA soldier William Wolfe, who died in the shoot-out, and states she will continue the terrorist fight.

September 18, 1975

Patricia Hearst and the Harrises are captured by the FBI in San Francisco.

March 20, 1976

Patricia Hearst is found guilty on both counts of her federal indictment stemming from the robbery of the Hibernia Bank.

SYPNOPSES OF THE SEVEN SLA TAPES

SLA Tape 1

In the first tape Cinque identifies himself as Field Marshal General of the Symbionese Liberation Army and defines the mission of the SLA as giving power back to the people. Cinque lists the holdings of the Hearst Corporation. He identifies the Hearsts as oppressors and the kidnapping as a retaliation against their exploitation. Field Marshal Cinque demands that the Hearsts show repentance in the form of a food program for the needy. He describes Patricia's condition as satisfactory, but threatens to execute her should the ransom demands not be followed to the letter. Patricia states that she is all right, but kept blindfolded. She requests that everyone calm down, not attempt to rescue her by force, and take the demands of the SLA seriously. Patricia identifies herself as a prisoner of war, comparable to the captured SLA soldiers, Remiro and Little. She expresses her desire to be released quickly.

SLA Tape 2

Patricia attempts to clear up the confusion on the specifications of the SLA for the food program. She emphasizes that everyone should believe she is alive, for it would give the FBI an excuse to enter the SLA hideout with their guns firing. Patricia views herself as a symbol of retaliation by the exploited and states that the SLA operation demonstrated that needy people could and should be fed. She requests that her mother not wear a black dress, as she is alive and anxious to return home.

SLA Tape 3

Cinque labels the Hearst's food distribution gesture as insincere. He continues his assessment of Hearst Corporation holdings in detail and accuses the Hearsts of inhumanity. Cinque states that the government is a dictatorship with laws that only serve to imprison its citizens. He goes on to list specific instructions for the distribution of the food and demands four million dollars be added to the already pledged two million. Cinque threatens to execute Patricia should any attempt be made to rescue her. General Field Marshal Cinque warns the people to be wary of government propaganda. He describes himself as one who was once oppressed, but is now in the superior position.

SLA Tape 4

Gelina begins the tape with demands that stolen property be returned to the people. She compares the "sincere" actions of the SLA with the "insincere" actions of the Hearsts. Gelina states that the FBI is trying to kill Patricia and that the government performs such sacrifices to kill freedom fighters. She demands national broadcast time for the two SLA prisoners. In this tape Patricia begins her accusations that her family does not really care about her safe release. She does not fear the SLA now, but rather her parents' indifference and the murderous intentions of the FBI. Patricia describes her family as protectors of their own interests. She feels that the news media are also against her and that the food program is a disaster. She requests that various members of her family and friends speak up in her defense and not take the "out of my hands" attitude of her father or the weak-willed stance of her mother. Patricia reveals that she has begun reading SLA literature and is even learning how to use a gun to protect herself from the FBI who has much to gain by her death. She demands that national broadcast time be provided for the two SLA prisoners and herself due to the scope of the kidnapping incident. Other members of the SLA, including Fahizah and Cinque, make very brief comments.

SLA Tape 5

In this tape, Patricia announces her decision to stay with the SLA. She denies being brainwashed, stating that she has changed and grown, and is now in love with the revolutionary cause. Patricia continues to demonstrate some measure of her connectedness to her fiancé, Steven Weed, expressing sympathy for his harassment by the FBI, but her parents are accused of deceiving her, the SLA and the people. She labels her father a liar, one who is knowledgeable of an impending corporate movement which would eliminate unneeded people from the work force, and one who only serves his own needs, quite willing to go along with the sacrifice of his own daughter. Patricia reveals that she was given the name "Tania" by the SLA, and that she has transformed her hate into a fight for freedom against the corporate state.

William Harris (Teko) presents his first entry on this tape. After identifying himself, he states that white men should cease their oppressive actions and join the SLA in their struggle to defeat the "slave masters." He goes on to promote revolutionary violence, claiming it is wrong to wait for backing from larger groups with the necessary skills for a revolution. Nancy Ling Perry (Fahizah) presents her first lengthy entry. She speaks of liberating the oppressed, and resisting the "disease of bourgeois mentality." Cinque is portrayed as a great leader who loves the people, and therefore an individual to be protected from the police, whom she says are intent on eliminating black leaders. She states that the people must strike the first blow against the merciless police.

Cinque is the last entry on the tape. He presents an enemies list consisting of names and physical descriptions of people he orders to be shot on sight. Cinque also announces that Patricia has been given her freedom, but refuses to leave. He states that no other kidnappings will take place, as it is evident that the corporate state is willing to sacrifice its own members. Cinque closes by sending his love to his children and playing the SLA national anthem.

SLA Tape 6

Cinque opens by describing the details of the SLA's Hibernia Bank robbery and explaining why it was necessary to shoot two persons. He follows this explanation by analyzing a current police investigation in California, labeled the Zebra Operation. Cinque believes the operation is constructed to create a race war and thus to prevent the organization of all oppressed people. He reasons that the search of black homes is the means to disarm the people, and that police identification cards are a method of classifying blacks by an FBI code. The Zebra Operation is portrayed ultimately as an attempt to assassinate Cinque because he is the teacher of the oppressed.

Teko's entry is essentially a repetition and support of Cinque's statements. He adds that white people are already enslaved by the present authorities and that it is time to fight, not talk. Black people are praised for their strength and determination and told that an army of all races is forming to fight the oppression of the government. Patricia, calling herself Tania, begins her entry with an account of the bank robbery and gives added emphasis to the nature of her participation (e.g., "my gun was loaded . . . "). She justifies the robbery as aiding the people. The Hearsts and Steven Weed are referred to as pigs. Patricia continues in her belief that the FBI will attempt to kill her if they get the opportunity. Brainwashing is again denied and statements of her status as a soldier in the People's Army are made.

SLA Tape 7

Teko opens the presentation by addressing a number of revolutionary groups. In a rather detailed manner, he relates the shoplifting incident at the sporting goods store. He interprets the shoot-out in Los Angeles as a heroic act by the SLA and a cowardly act by the police.

Teko feels that the authorities are attempting to defame Cinque by claiming he had committed suicide during the shoot-out. A promise to continue the fight for freedom is made. Emily Harris (Yolanda) introduces herself on this tape. She reviews the killing of SLA members and states that the repression of the present military-industrial state makes people feel powerless and breeds resistance. Whites must prove their willingness to fight and should remember that the police will kill them as well as minority groups. Patricia is the last entry. She provides a eulogy for each of the SLA dead. Her love for the recently deceased William Wolfe (Kujoe) is expressed and her discussions with him on the subject of her parents' inadequacy are described. She explains that since they were being trained as leaders, it is wrong to assume that they are now leaderless. Patricia describes herself as reborn. After a short review of the options before her of where she might live, Patricia pledges her willingness to continue the revolution.

Analysis of the Tapes

During February of 1974, after the release of the third SLA tape, an initial analysis of the contents of the first three tapes was made for the FBI. Employing the methods of psycholinguistic analysis, an attempt was made to identify the age, race, birthplace and backgrounds of the unidentified subjects making those tapes. In addition, the report made predictions concerning the safety of Patricia Hearst, the personalities of the SLA members and suggestions for negotiation strategies. The description given in that report for Cinque, before he had been positively identified as Donald DeFreeze, stated in part that:

> Cinque either has children of his own or is close to someone who does. He is clearly black and in his middle to late twenties. He has probably spent time in jail or been involved with the criminal courts. He is poor and is probably not part of any university radical group. He is distinctly middle class in outlook. He **respects** the powerful. He is painfully incapable of decisive action, easily led and docile. He is the central personality of the SLA faction holding Patricia; he is the action focus of the group, the doer not the thinker. He is intellectually inferior to Gelina, who is probably his wife and second in the group pecking order. He has difficulty manipulating complex notions.
>
> The critical problem in dealing with the SLA is their determination to commit suicide by establishing the conditions under which their destruction at the hands of someone else is inevi-

table. Even Patricia has been drawn into the mutual suicide pact. Cinque is acting the dominant male role, posing for the women of the group. He maintains dominance so long as he is seen as the source of expertise in crime. Attempts must be made to assert influence over Patricia's suggestability and to bring her back to identification with the outside world rather than the distorted reality of the SLA.

In the plethora of speculations regarding the motivations of the terrorist, it is ironically tragic that quantitative analyses languish. If we are to control the increasing expressions of violence which threaten our society, it is imperative that we seek every technology at our disposal to understand the nature and character of those who would use terror as their weapon. What better source could we hope for in our understanding of the SLA than their own words?

During the time Patricia was held hostage, joined the SLA and eluded the law, my student, Dr. Thomas Pasquale, and I were busy analyzing the tapes in minute detail by means of the computer. Dr. Pasquale's doctoral dissertation on this case is more than 400 pages in length. Using the messages produced by the six SLA members who vented their dissatisfactions to the world at large, we attempted to make a general description of the content of these communications.

The first step was to construct a computer dictionary which contained a large number of word and phrase entries organized around categories of importance in terrorist acts. Thus, for example, the category of **DESTRUCTION** in the dictionary represented all those phrases and terms such as **kill**, **bomb**, **blow-away**, which might occur in the texts. The computer dictionary is able to ascertain the difference between different meanings for the same word by scanning the way the word or phrase is used in the text. The word **pig**, for example, which is so often seen in such messages can be initially assigned to the category of **DENIGRATION-LOW STATUS** rather than as a farm animal by examination of the preceding words for membership in the category **INSTITUTION**. Hence, **fascist pig** and **corporate pig** are people while **delicious pig** and **roasted pig** are animals. Further tests of more distant words surrounding the ambiguous word are then made so that "the fascists will be **roast pigs** when we're through" is correctly assigned. The construction of such a dictionary takes considerable time and ingenuity. Once constructed however, messages can be scanned by the computer and its dictionary in, literally, microseconds.

Mr. Richard Velde, then Deputy Administrator of the Law Enforcement Assistance Administration (LEAA) and now Director of LEAA, in his testimony before the House Committee on Internal Security has said of this approach:

> A proposal currently being reviewed and which is receiving serious consideration is one by Professor Murray S. Miron, Professor of Psycholinguistics at Syracuse University. This project, entitled "Semantic Analyses of Threat Communications," would seek to achieve an understanding of the personality dynamics of those individuals who employ threats of violence or property damage as the central part of their criminal behavior. Threats and subsequent behavior would be studied to form the basis for a threat analysis dictionary. Such a dictionary could be used to automatically scan threat communications as they are received in an attempt to identify the predicted outcome and courses of action contained within the threat. As a result, police responsiveness to particularly threatening communications could be improved markedly. (Congressional Record, July 1974)

For the purposes of examining the SLA communications, we constructed a dictionary of 85 categories which successfully classified approximately 60% of all the significant word occurrences of the messages. Some of our work in devising the dictionary had already been done by other researchers working on other applications of the content analysis problem. Phillip Stone, of Harvard University, and his colleagues, and J. Phillip Miller of St. Louis University, particularly, have spent much of their professional lifetimes refining this approach to the understanding of language. The 845 categories of the *Threat Analysis Dictionary* we employed represent a composite of categories drawn from the work of these other researchers plus categories of our own devising related specifically to the problems of threat.

As the text is scanned by the computer dictionary, the frequencies of occurrences of words assigned to each category are printed as a profile of the content of the message. The next step is to take these frequencies in each category and relate them to every other category in order to detect patterns of similarities of category use. These patterns, in turn, are then examined by the computer to determine the essential attributes or central themes contained in the message. The pattern of themes is, in every regard, an explanation of the nature of the message.

When this procedure is applied to the SLA communications, three dominant themes emerge. In order of prominence, the messages all contained themes of **IMPOTENCE-DENIAL, DESTRUCTIVE REACTION** and **AFFILIATIVE NEEDS**. The accompanying illustration (see Figure

5.1) displays these thematic dimensions of the message content as the coordinates of a space within which each of the communicators is arrayed. Each of the SLA members exhibits differing prominence of these three themes at different times, but all of them share the identical pattern. The dimensions represent quantitative yardsticks of the principal aspects of the content of their messages to the world at large. They are the dimensions of **content** and nature of the words they employed.

Impotence-denial, the most prominent of these dimensions, reflects the commonly shared perceptions of powerlessness which all of the members of the SLA manifested – actors, responding to weakness by denying that weakness in the rhetoric of power. These weak, acting as if they were strong, chose to react to their circumstances by destruction of the system in which they found themselves powerless. But, significantly, they also manifest an intense need for the affiliative support of each other and the larger society which they would attack. Thus, from feelings of impotence, the SLA sought to deny their weakness by acts of destruction which they perceived as enlisting the sympathies and in affiliation with the needs of others whom they saw as equally helpless. Cinque and Gelina in tapes 3 and 4, respectively, can be seen from the display to have manifested far greater impotence than any of their cohorts. Patricia in tape 4, the tape in which she declares that she no longer fears the SLA but, rather, the FBI whom she believes is determined to kill her, manifests the greatest need for protective affiliation.

This tape marks the clear beginnings of the delusional identification with her aggressors which was to eventually culminate in the bank robbery. From this point she moves increasingly closer to the content themes of the other members of the SLA until in the last tape, tape 7, in her eulogy of her dead comrades, she evidences greater destructive reaction than even Cinque had during the entire odyssey. She and the surviving Harrises, Teko and Yolanda, speak from the farthest corner of the space of maximum impotence and maximum destructiveness. It seems evident that had Patricia been rescued at that point at which she was most needful of protective affiliation she might not have chosen the destructive affiliation of the SLA. The analysis also makes it clear that the destructive manifestations of Patricia and the Harrises augered continuing revolutionary activity following the death of their comrades.

We believe that these dimensions can be applied to other terrorist groups. In fact, we boldly suggest that these central themes can be applied to a wide range of communication behavior. The essential

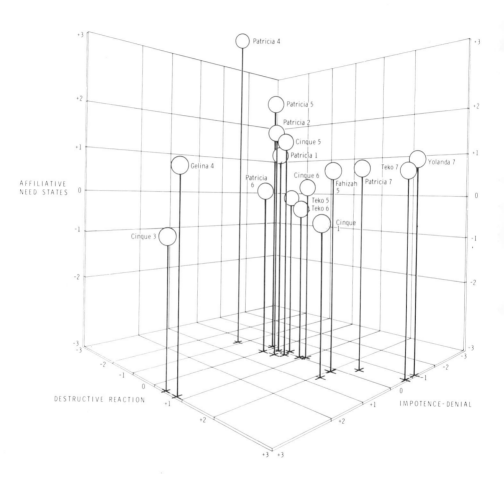

Figure 5.1: Content Dimensions of SLA Members as Taken from Taped Messages

characterization of what one means by a terrorist act, the illegitimate use of forceful coercion as against legitimized and sanctioned force, may well reside in the degree to which the act is motivated by perceptions of impotence. The normal individual copes with his feelings of powerlessness by denying that powerlessness. We found that powerlessness is closely associated with denial, that the two invariably are connected. If the insensitivity of the bureaucracy leaves us feeling helpless, we avoid the bureaucracy. We may also choose to conform by accepting our powerlessness. But when denial of our powerlessness is not sufficient to cope with increasing assaults upon our perceptions of our own worth, some may choose to lash out in angry, destructive resentment. Those without any vestige of socially sanctioned power may choose to destroy the society which has denied them that power. But, additionally, what we found was that these groups crave the support and approval of affiliation, of belonging. It is affiliation which gives them identity and meaning. If they cannot be Americans, some may choose to be liberation armies, complete with rank, status and comradeship.

For the society, for our culture at this point in our brief history, these interpretations are significant. The SLA may have taught us more than they intended. Unless we understand the destructive cry of such groups for the dignity of significance, the cry of all of us for the recognition of our just worth, destructiveness can be expected to continue to plague us.

6 / The Media, "Shrinks" and Other Civilians

At several points in this book, we have touched upon some of the problems involved in the relationship between the officer and those civilians who may play a role in a hostage situation. This chapter will attempt to address some of these problems in greater detail. Although we consider the hostage situation to be a law enforcement operation, it is clear that the law enforcement presence must operate within the context of public attitudes as both represented and shaped by the news media. Additionally, it is also clear that these situations may require cooperation between the law enforcement officer and psychiatrists or psychologists who typically know as little about law enforcement as the officer knows of their profession.

Not uncommonly, the use of such expertise may be accompanied by suspicion, hostility and the sort of intellectual gamesmanship which stem from the distorted stereotypes each profession has of the other. On one occasion, while I was patrolling with an officer of the Syracuse force, the officer was dispatched to render assistance on an ambulance call. When we arrived, the ambulance personnel were attempting to aid a severely intoxicated man who was bleeding profusely from a head wound he had sustained as a result of a fall. The ambulance crew was having no success. The man steadfastly refused to accept medical help. His alcohol level was sufficiently high to assure that he was in little pain despite the patently severe nature of his wound. After strenuous rejection of their considerable cajoling, the ambulance crew started to leave. The officer quietly asked them to wait for a moment longer outside the house. Then he and I (Dr. Miron) also left to sit in the patrol car. Moments later, as the officer had fully anticipated, the man struck his wife and stormed out of the house screaming obscenities. Once outside, the officer immediately arrested him for public intoxication and had him taken in the waiting ambulance for emergency treatment.

When we arrived at the hospital, the emergency room physician after examining the head wound turned to the officer and disgustedly asked whether he had broken his night stick when he had hit the man. The officer responded, matter-of-factly, that he probably would need a new one and turned to make out his arrest report. Dumbfounded and angry, I asked the officer why he had appeared to agree with the physician's grossly unjust conclusion when in fact the officer had not only not struck the citizen but had acted solely out of humanitarian concern. His reply was simple. He had concluded long ago that nothing would convince those like this physician that cops could be human and had even stopped feeling angry about it. Such is the stuff of stereotypes.

THE MEDIA

The news media also bear their share of misconceptions about the law enforcement officer. They often assume that the close knit law enforcement community will attempt to conceal anything which may be unfavorable to themselves. As a consequence, they may interpret attempts to control media coverage of an incident as an effort to cover up something. A number of other complaints have been raised about the behavior of some media personnel in hostage situations. On occasion, it is claimed, they have gotten caught up in the excitement of the event, lost their objectivity, leading, for example, to poor judgment in decisions about what to cover live and for how long. Or they have been too zealous, seeking "scoops" in a kind of competitive journalism which may endanger hostages, police or themselves by reporting police tactics, by tying up phone lines, by harrassing police personnel, by inopportunely telephoning perpetrators, and by similar actions. And more. Media personnel have, it is said, allowed themselves to be used as propaganda conduits, as vehicles to bring political or idealogical pressure to bear upon others, and as quasi- or actual hostages. At times, hostage situation journalism has been described as including the use of scare headlines and sensationalism, and as perpetuating rumors. Perhaps most serious, by their behavior and very presence, the media have been charged with encouraging the occurrence of the antisocial behaviors which they are purporting to objectively report.

These are numerous and quite serious accusations. It is to the very considerable credit of American journalism that they have for the most part listened openly to these charges and, in response, have become engaged in a strenuous, in-depth consideration of both the merits of the accusations and alternative remedial actions. At philosphical, ethical and operational levels, a number of specific, constructive steps have been proposed. The National News Council urges areas of self-restraint, use of judicious coverage and careful editing. They also stress the dangers of seeking interviews with perpetrators while the event is still in progress. One journalist, himself a hostage in the Hanafi takeover, has proposed that newsmen receive special training in how to cope with terrorist crises; that each metropolitan area set up a committee of editors who could agree on declaring and enforcing a "news media emergency" in which certain everyday journalistic rules might be self-suspended; and that terrorist incidents involving hostages be handled by the news media in ways similar to kidnappings and wars — in which there are usually agreements about types of materials to be published at will, on a delayed basis or not at all.

A journalism group in California has developed guidelines which include: elimination of airing of rumors and unverified statements; avoiding the reporting of trivial statements; care about use of cameras, bright lights or microphones that may encourage exhibitionism; avoidance of scare headlines; using only experienced reporters at the scene; emphasizing in dispatches the efforts by law enforcement personnel to deal with the situation; discouragement of journalistic competition. A Louisville newspaper, in its guidelines, emphasized that the decision to publish specific information about the hostage event, whenever possible, ought to be made by the paper's most senior editor available, in consultation with top police officials.

Several discussions of media-hostage-police problems similarly emphasize a consultation solution, one in which media and law enforcement personnel strive together for reciprocal relationships of benefit to all. This is a solution which is very attractive to us and one whose dimensions we will seek to develop more fully below. We do wish to note first, however, that constructive attempts to identify and operationalize an optimal role for the media in hostage situations have been a serious goal of police personnel also. Perhaps the best example of this is a recent statement by Lt. Frank Bolz, head of the New York Police Department Hostage Negotiation Squad. Bolz, a remarkably experienced and successful hostage negotiator, proposes that there be:

1. Adequate police-media precrisis meetings to develop guidelines and specific procedures for in-crisis collaboration.

2. Energetic effort by the police to keep the media informed and up-to-date on all major aspects of the hostage event.

3. No communication by the media of police tactics either planned or in progress.

4. No direct telephone access for media personnel to perpetrators.

5. Police-media cooperation on tactics designed to secure release of hostages, e.g., promising to meet the perpetrator's request for a prime time interview, but only after hostages are released.

As noted earlier, we are particularly optimistic about the value of precrisis preparation and collaboration between police and media personnel as a major route for dealing with many of the problems highlighted above. The key is that of understanding the roles, restrictions and principles of the participants. As the later chapters of this book point out, role rehearsals provide an effective tool for understanding the circumstances of the participants in negotiation. One need not ask the media or a psychiatrist to role play the besieged officer at a hostage scene or that the officer play their roles. It is often possible to effect the understanding which derives from such role reversal by simply trying one's best to understand the positions of those who might otherwise become adversaries. We believe that this requires that each participant disclose as fully as possible his operating principles and procedures.

Specifically, in discussions taking place prior to actual hostage or other crisis events, the news media should be made aware of the planning and procedures which your jurisdiction has adopted for crisis contingencies along with their reasons and purposes. The media, in turn, should be asked to detail their guidelines with respect to coverage of such incidents. If they have not adopted such guidelines or if there is apparent conflict in the procedures on either side, these problems should be resolved **before** the crisis catches both of the parties either unprepared or in conflict. At the scene of a crisis, there should be an officer who, as a result of such prior discussion is respected and trusted by the media, and who is designated to provide liason with the working press. It does not seem unreasonable to us, in view of our opinion that such crises are under the lawful control of the authorities, that representatives of the working press be required to obtain identification before being allowed at the scene. Granting of such ID can serve to limit the number of media representatives to those who have participated in the planning discussions.

Imitation Effects

An exceedingly important aspect of concern regarding the role of the media in hostage situations asks the question: What is the relationship between news coverage of such incidents and the later occurrence of other similar incidents? Dr. David Phillips, a sociologist at the University of California, has published two papers which bear directly on this question. Phillips first examined the fluctuations in the number of suicides in the United States and Great Britain following publicity given to suicides of prominent personages. He found that there was an increase in the suicide rate following publication of such prominent suicides, and that the increase in the general suicide rate was positively correlated with the amount of such publicity. He concluded that the relationship was to be accounted for on the basis of an imitative effect caused by the news stories. In the second study, Phillips examined the relationship between publicized suicide stories and the number of motor vehicle fatalities. He argued that if car accidents may have a suicidal component they, like his earlier conclusion regarding direct suicides, should also increase following publicity of prominent suicides.

Using a combined index of the total circulation of each of five California newspapers and the number of days in which these newspapers contained a front-page suicide account, Phillips found that there was indeed a significant relationship between the amount of publicity and the fluctuations of the accident rate following the news stories. On the average, Phillips reports a 9.12% increase in the number of accidents during the week following publication of a prominent suicide. When he examined only those suicides which received more than the median publicity devoted to the suicides of his sample, the increase in motor vehicle accidents reached as high as 18.84%. Neither of these increases can be accounted for on the basis of chance fluctuations in the accident rates of Phillip's data, and since he attempted to match the changes in accident rates following the suicide stories with control times during which there were no publicized suicides, he concludes that the relationship is causal in character. Although the methodology of such essentially correlative studies is somewhat controversial, the results of these two studies are, at the very least, provocative. They imply that there can be both direct and indirect stimulation of suicides as a consequence of publicity regarding other suicides.

This conclusion well fits the common-sense observation of the high similarity and wave-like occurrence of recent hostage incidents.

We examined the total coverage devoted to hostage-taking, barricade and terrorism incidents during the period from October 1, 1976 through February 28, 1977 as reported in *The New York Times*. During this period there is a clear, progressive increase in the total newspaper coverage of such incidents. Obviously, the amount of newspaper space devoted to such incidents is dependent upon the number of incidents during the period. However, an examination of the content of the demands made by the perpetrators certainly suggests that they are, among other motivations, determined to capture newspaper headlines. If, as we have already suggested, there is a suicidal component associated with these more bizarre forms of crimes, Phillips' conclusion may well directly extend to the incidence of hostage-taking acts.

None of the foregoing, even if such an imitative conclusion were to be considered correct, can be construed as an argument for not reporting such incidents. The news media's argument that any form of censorship whether internally or externally initiated only acts to undermine the essential informational functions of an independent press and to create suspicion of other manipulation is certainly sound. But there are alternatives intermediate between reporting or not reporting such incidents. Much of the coverage which has been made in the past tends to focus on descriptions of the act. Relatively little coverage is given to the background. The very objectivity of these descriptions endows the incident with a sterility which diminishes the heinousness of the crime. Most of these offenders are childlike in their intemperateness, confused, destructive and ineffectual. Headlines such as "ARMED TERRORISTS HOLD HOSTAGES, CITY IN TERROR," make these angry children bigger than they are. The truth of the matter might be closer to "GUNMEN'S TANTRUM SEEKS TO CAUSE FEAR." One does not emulate acts which one considers unworthy or unheroic.

ASSISTANCE FROM MENTAL HEALTH EXPERTS

With respect to the use of psychiatric assistance, our advice is similar. One should not expect to be able to call in some expert for help without previous discussions of what it is that he will be asked to do or under what conditions he will be required to function. There is nothing more comical than the scene of some psychiatrist being instructed on how to don a bullet-proof vest. Dr. Schlossberg tells the anecdote of how his New York City Crisis Force attempted to contact psychiatrists for advice in the Brooklyn Sporting Goods siege. After explaining the nature of the crisis and asking for psychological suggestions on negotiating strategies, these experts responded with the advice that the police should use tear gas. The police obviously knew how to use tear gas and knew that it would be ineffective in this situation, but the psychiatrists perhaps as much as the police assumed that the other had the magical solution.

Dr. Thomas Szasz, a psychiatrist who has a reputation of being an iconoclast, recently suggested that psychiatrists have no business being involved in such hostage incidents. Reacting to the negotiation attempts of Dr. Dirk Mulder in the two South Moluccan incidents of 1976 and 1977, Szasz asked in a letter to the editor of the *New York Times*: "What do psychiatrists know about terrorism that anyone else doesn't?" His startling answer to his own question was that they either do not know anything, or that they are themselves terrorists and therefore well-qualified. Szasz states:

> Why do psychiatrists negotiate with terrorists? What do psychiatrists know about terrorism that anyone else doesn't? In my opinion, there can be only two answers to these questions. One is that psychiatrists have no special expertise in terrorism, and using psychiatrists to negotiate with terrorists is simply a part of our contemporary craze of psychiatrizing all human situations that involve conflict. The other is that psychiatrists have a special expertise in terrorism because they are themselves terrorists.

This scathing denunciation should not be dismissed out of hand. Nor, as psychologists ourselves, do we feel that Szasz means to exculpate that profession from his indictment. Many who read Szasz's statement will find confirmation of what they already believed to be true of all such experts. But it seems to us that while Szasz has correctly raised an issue that must be addressed and that must be taken into account whenever such expertise is employed, his polemic conclusion is exaggeratively false. The role of any psychological expert at the scene of a crisis is, at best, an ambiguous one. He is typically not a law enforcement officer, except in those rare instances like that of Dr. Schlossberg who is both a psychologist and a police officer with more than 14 years experience.

The civilian expert who is rarely paid for his services is thus not "employed" by anyone. To whom does he owe his allegiance, whose interests can he be expected to serve? If injured at the scene of a crisis, would the city provide his widow and his children the benefits to which a police officer would be entitled? If asked to sign a release form, what effect does such knowledge of lack of official responsibility have upon his approach to what he is asked to do? If called to a scene for assistance and advice, what authority does such a civilian have over decisions which he might believe to be dangerous to himself or others? Or conversely, what weight should be placed upon the advice of such an expert? In the early 1977 Dutch hostage incident, Dr. Mulder, according to his own account, was instrumental in deciding that the psychological climate of those on the train required that the siege be ended by the assault which resulted in the deaths of two of the hostages and six of the South Moluccan terrorists. In an interview with *Medical World News*, Mulder said he saw signs of rebellion against the terrorist leader's authority on the part of the other terrorists, indications of what was believed to be the possibility that the hostages were planning their own assault on their captors, and finally that the stresses on the hostages could produce more medical complications like the heart attack suffered by one of the captives. We do not know precisely how these conclusions were reached, but we do know that Dr. Mulder's medical and psychiatric opinions must have played some significant role in the surprise decision to assault the train.

We do not have easy answers to these difficult questions. But one conclusion appears to be inevitable. Until the questions of to whom the expert owes his allegiance and who it is that he represents, are resolved, we believe that it is wisest **not** to use civilian experts as direct, "face-to-face" negotiators. We believe that their role should be restricted to that of advisor and observer. Further, law enforcement agencies should be made more aware that there are no magic psychological bullets which will solve these situations. Psychological expertise should be viewed as simply one additional source of input into the decision-making process which is the ultimate responsibility of the law enforcement agency.

In summary, it is clear that the difficult job confronting law enforcement personnel faced with hostage situations can be greatly aided when there is effective, preplanned police collaboration with media and mental health personnel. Both types of civilians have their own legitimate needs, responsibilities and rights. At times, these conflict with the equally legitimate position of the police. In this chapter we have sought to explore a number of the sources of potential police-civilian conflict, and emerging means for their solution. The energetic manner in which both police and civilians are contributing to these solutions is a most hopeful sign for their eventual resolution.

7 / Hostage Negotiation Procedures

I. SAFETY

1. **Sufficient Personnel**
   Make certain sufficient personnel are both trained in hostage management strategy and tactics and available in adequate numbers for a hostage situation.*

2. **Chain of Command**
   The hostage management area, inner and outer perimeter personnel, fire-power, communications and related resources must be controlled and coordinated by a single source.

3. **Media Cooperation**
   Influence media, if possible, so no mention is made of tactical plans and resources.

4. **Communication**
   Maintain communication among responding personnel.

5. **Identification of Personnel**
   All inner perimeter personnel must be readily identifiable.

   Police and nonpolice (e.g., "outside" negotiation advisors) personnel should wear clothing whose colors, markings or other charac-

---

*See Chapters eight and nine for a complete discussion of negotiator training.

istics clearly identify them as law enforcement personnel. The hostage management situation may deteriorate suddenly, as when a hostage is unexpectedly killed, and rapid, substantial firepower may quickly be put into use. Under such circumstances, in which firepower must be used with rapid judgment and acute perception, especially clear identification of inner perimeter personnel is obviously highly desirable.

6. Negotiator Position
The negotiator should be physically near the perpetrator, but secure enough that he won't become a hostage himself.

Where and how the negotiator is positioned should reflect both concern with his personal safety and the importance of his establishing rapport with the perpetrator. He should **not** be face-to-face with the perpetrator, but should be close enough that he can communicate directly by voice without aid of bullhorn or similar equipment if possible. This may mean communication through a closed door or around a corner. This physical arrangement will often not be possible, in which case telephone communication is the desirable alternative.

7. Hostage Identification
Make sure there IS a hostage.

By use of binoculars, telephone or other means, verify the fact that hostages exist. If possible, ascertain their number and identity. If possible, seek opportunity to actually see the hostages. When you are able to do so, remember prominent physical characteristics of hostages and communicate these descriptions to all inner perimeter personnel. Such communication minimizes chances of confusion by responding personnel of hostages and perpetrators. In doing so, remember not to rely on clothing, glasses or similar items in your description of hostages, as such items are easily switched by perpetrators.

8. Perpetrator Requests for Others
Do not fulfill perpetrator requests to bring relatives or friends to the scene.

The presence of the perpetrator's relatives or friends adds unpredictable elements to a situation you are trying to control and make at least moderately predictable. Such friends and relatives may be employed as allies by the perpetrator, or he may use them as additional hostages, or his purpose in seeking their presence may be as an audience in front of which he may enact violent and sometimes suicidal acts. In none of these examples is your ability to successfully manage the resolution of the hostage incident increased. Thus, the request should generally not be fulfilled. Your optimal way of dealing with the request will probably be to stall, to indicate you have to seek approval for it up the chain of command, etc., rather than to refuse outright. We must note, however, as with all rules there are potential exceptions. In the Indianapolis incident, the negotiators effectively used Kiritsis' brother at one point in the negotiations (see chapter three).

9. Avoid Show of Force
Avoid a show of force, especially when a single perpetrator is involved.

A visible display of S.W.A.T., Special Reaction Team or similar groups of highly armed and numerous personnel may provide the spark which ignites the short fuse of violence in the unstable perpetrator. That is, a massing of visible firepower may result in exactly the opposite of the deterrent effect intended. Whether due to fear, enhanced chance for glory, or as a play-to-the-audience effect, a show of force may lead to killing of hostages. Some authorities have suggested that a show of force is a useful hostage management technique in prison settings, as a means of acting before the group consolidates, and when several perpetrators — especially political terrorists — are involved, as the show of force may weaken the commitment of one or more of the perpetrators.

10. Non-Negotiables
Do not negotiate for new weapons, alcohol, narcotics or other items likely to increase the threat to hostage or negotiator safety.

Such items will at times be included among perpetrator demands. Like requests for the presence of relatives or other people who may become additional hostages, requests for weapons or other danger-increasing items are best dealt with by stalling, appealing to chain of command delays, and using several other negotiating techniques described later in this chapter.

11. Avoid Shifts of Location
If at all possible, avoid movement of the perpetrator and hostages to another location.

The perpetrator at a hostage scene may demand that he and his hostages be moved elsewhere. Most often this demand will be for purposes of escape, e.g., demands to be taken to an airport and readied plane. Sometimes the demand is to a place where certain other people reside, e.g., mother, wife, girlfriend. Other movement demands are sometimes made. In all instances, agreeing with such demands is to be avoided if at all possible. Movement of perpetrator and hostage severely diminishes the control you have established at the hostage scene. New people, new resources for the perpetrator, and new unfavorable turns of events may all enter the scene if you permit it to shift at the demand of the perpetrator.

12. **Safety Instructions for Hostages**
If it is possible to communicate by any direct means with the hostages, provide them with the following suggestions designed to increase their safety:
1. Stay as calm and alert as possible.
2. Do not try to fight with perpetrators, avoid provoking them.
3. Try to build a positive relationship with the perpetrator.
4. Try to be as real a person to perpetrators as possible (share thoughts on your hopes, plans, family, problems.)
5. Follow perpetrator instructions to the extent possible.
6. Avoid political discussions.
7. Eat food offered you.
8. Be aware that many of the effects of drugs are psychological.
9. Stay face-to-face with armed perpetrators.

II. INFORMATION TO BE OBTAINED

1. **Information about the Perpetrator**
Relevant information about the perpetrator should be gathered as completely and rapidly as possible.
To help the negotiator determine both the tone and content of his statements to the perpetrator, the following information about the perpetrator will be valuable:
1. Characteristics: names, number, age, sex, size, physical condition.
2. Background: race, ethnic group, politics.
3. Personality: degree of rationality, tolerance for ambiguity, aggression potential.
4. Prior crimes and police record.
5. Specific details of present crime.
6. Purpose of hostage act: criminal, terrorist, mentally disturbed.
7. Intelligence.
8. Emotional state.
9. Any at-the-scene behavior.
10. Stated reasons for hostage-taking (motivation and plans).

11. Nature and amount of arms.
12. Specialized skills.
13. Special affiliations.
14. Unusual habits.

2. **Information about the Hostages**
Relevant information about the hostages should be gathered as completely and rapidly as possible.
To help the negotiator determine both the tone and content of his statements to the perpetrator, the following information about the hostages will be valuable:
1. Characteristics: number, age, sex, size.
2. Background: race, ethnic group.
3. Aggression potential.
4. Intelligence.
5. Emotional state.
6. Medical problems or special requirements.

3. **Information about the Hostage Site**
Ascertain the following about the hostage site:
1. Safe observation positions.
2. Escape routes.
3. Safest approach routes.
4. Any telephones present.
5. Amount of space, number of rooms, ventilation.
6. Food, water.
7. Method required for effective gassing.

III. THE NEGOTIATOR

1. **Optimal Negotiator Characteristics**
1. Interpersonal sensitivity.
2. Cognitive complexity.
3. Tolerance for ambiguity.
4. Positive self-concept.
5. Low authoritarianism.
6. Interviewing experience.
7. Past experience in stressful situations.
8. Verbal skills.
9. Flexibility, especially under pressure.
10. Work history with many different types of perpetrators.
11. Belief in the power of **verbal** persuasion.
12. Conciliation, compromise, bargaining skills.

13. Mature appearance.
14. Apparent rank of patrolman* (even a sergeant may be seen as a final decision maker).
15. Good physical condition.
16. Familiarity with the ideology of perpetrator if a terrorist is involved.

2. Undesirable Negotiator Characteristics
1. Strong belief in physical force, power and toughness.
2. Over-conformity and formality.
3. Difficulty expressing personal feelings.
4. Machismo orientation.
5. High authoritarianism.
6. Rigidity or inflexibility.
7. Poor verbal skills.
8. Tendency to project own feelings on others.
9. Tendency to avoid introspection.
10. Nonvaried work history.
11. Poor bargaining skills.
12. Immature appearance.
13. Poor physical condition.
14. Unfamiliarity with ideology of perpetrator.

3. Negotiator Styles

Table 7.1
Negotiator Styles and Strategies

Negotiator	Win-Lose Battler	Equalizer	Soft-Bargainer
Apparent Negotiating Strategies	Forcing	Problem-Solving Compromise	Giving-In

An Equalizer negotiator style, in which Problem-Solving and Compromise are the negotiating strategies preferred, is the negotiator style to be recommended for hostage situations. Unsatisfactory negotiating outcomes are much more likely when the negotiator's preferred style of operation is too forceful (the Win-Lose Battler) or too gentle (the Soft-Bargainer).

---

*To insure perpetrator is aware that all decisions must be approved at other command levels.

IV. NEGOTIATING STRATEGIES

1. Initial Strategy

At the outset, contain and stabilize are your two goals. Avoid all precipitous acts.

Your initial negotiating strategy should seek to increase the predictability of the hostage scene and your control over it. Calming the agitated perpetrator and building rapport with him, both of which are discussed in detail later in this chapter, are your initial tactical goals. Precipitous acts, e.g., sudden and obvious movement of large numbers of men and equipment toward the perpetrator, will work opposite to your contain and stabilize purposes. Your ability to control the scene and begin implementing your negotiations will, of course, depend a great deal on your pre-event planning, negotiator training, and command efficiency at the scene.

2. Establish Problem-Solving Climate

Establish a problem-solving negotiating climate.

In all possible ways, communicate to the perpetrator your awareness that a problem exists, your desire to understand the problem and, in all reasonable ways possible, your willingness to help solve the problem. Establishing a problem-solving climate will mean trying to lead the perpetrator to believe he and you are working together in seeking problem solutions acceptable to both of you. Success in establishing this climate will mean considerable use of "we" and "us" (and not "you" versus "me"), considerable (and time-consuming) exploration of alternative problem solutions, and the likelihood of further development of negotiator-perpetrator rapport beyond that established by procedures described later. As other authorities have suggested, try to establish a climate in which you are both focusing upon defeating the problem, not each other. We agree with Schlossberg, whose overall negotiating strategy is:

> Our approach resembles crisis intervention therapy for suicidal people. You try to establish contact with the person, identify with him, find out his problem, and get him to look for another solution. . . . What we're looking for is time until his anxiety maybe abates and the negotiations appear to offer him an alternative course of action.

3. Establish Climate of Compromise

Seek to develop an atmosphere in which compromise is a major goal.

In seeking to create a climate of compromise, the negotiator communicates a give-and-take attitude, a willingness to bargain, an openness to yield on certain matters while holding firm on others. Each side, he makes clear, can gain something. The "something" for the negotiator, of course, is the release of the hostages.

4. **Avoid Forcing Climate**
   Minimize use of force or coercion.
   The negotiator using this strategy has also been described as the "win-lose battler." He is tough, rarely compromises, and has many of the traits and behaviors listed in Table 7.1 as undesirable negotiator characteristics. He will win some, but he will lose some also . . . too many. An aggressive, unyielding negotiator approach will needlessly threaten the lives of hostages and should be actively avoided.

5. **Avoid Use of "Soft-Bargainer" Climate**
   Avoid use of a soft-bargainer negotiating strategy.
   Just as some negotiators can be too tough, others can be too gentle. The negotiator who is too concerned with perpetrator feelings, too concerned with being accepted and well-liked, and too willing to yield to perpetrator demands will fail to bring the negotiations to a satisfactory conclusion.

6. **Strategy Varies with Perpetrator**
   Use the negotiating strategy which your pre-negotiating investigation reveals best fits the nature of the perpetrator involved.

Table 7.2
Negotiator Strategies and Types of Perpetrators

Criminal (Instrumental Behavior)	Terrorist	Psychotic (Expressive Behavior)
Emphasize Rational Techniques		Emphasize Emotional Techniques
a) Problem-Solving		a) Reflection of Feeling
b) Compromise		b) Restatement of Content

Optimal negotiator strategy and tactics will vary with the type of perpetrator. We call this "prescriptive negotiating." The criminal, who may take hostages to avoid capture after an unsuccessful robbery or other crime, has been described by several authorities as essentially rational and logical, and thus open to rational negotiating techniques.

These include direct attempts at problem solving and compromise. The mentally disturbed perpetrator is usually less accessible to appeals to reason. He is much more unpredictable and often closed to logical problem solving. The negotiator with such perpetrators is well-advised to focus on a more emotional negotiating strategy, in which he shows understanding, reflects perpetrator feelings, restates perpetrator content, and in other ways shows the perpetrator he is with him. The terrorist perpetrator presents a mixed picture in our view, he is "emotionally rational" and must be approached by means of joint rational and emotional negotiating techniques.

7. **Use of Force**
Use of force should be planned for, but implemented only as a last resort.

V. CALMING THE PERPETRATOR

1. **Show Understanding**
Attempt to calm the agitated perpetrator by showing understanding of his feelings.

By your words, tone of voice (and, if visible to the perpetrator) your facial expression and gestures, make it clear to the perpetrator that you accurately understand **what** he is feeling and **how strongly** he is feeling it. Some examples of calming attempts by showing understanding include, "You're really feeling very angry and upset at him," or, "What you just said is something you seem to feel very positive about."

2. **Modeling**
Attempt to calm the agitated perpetrator by displaying your own calmness to him.

By your words, tone of voice (and, if visible to the perpetrator) your facial expression and gestures, it clear to the perpetrator that you, the negotiator, are responding in a calm and controlled manner to the hostage incident. You can speak at a normal conversational level, at a slow and deliberate rate and if appropriate from a safety standpoint, you can sit down, remove your hat and behave in a variety of other ways to demonstrate calmness and the fact that a show of police force is not imminent. Since we are all likely to imitate people in authority, the negotiator's calmness will often have a direct calming effect on the agitated or highly emotional perpetrator.

3. **Reassurance**
Attempt to calm the agitated perpetrator by reassuring him.

In using modeling to calm the agitated perpetrator, the negotiator's own behavior serves as an example we hope the perpetrator will imitate. Use of reassurance takes the calming attempt a step further because the negotiator not only behaves calmly but, in addition, provides the perpetrator with reasons why he, too, should feel calmer. Examples of reassuring statements include: "We'll be able to work this out"; "I think we can deal with this a step at a time"; and, "I'm really interested in solving this with you."

4. **Encourage Ventilation**
   Attempt to calm the agitated perpetrator by encouraging him to talk.
   The negotiator is likely to be successful in calming a highly emotional perpetrator if he can be kept talking — about his demands, their background, complications, his hopes and so forth. It is quite difficult to remain highly emotional and at the same time answer questions, present information at length, and otherwise respond to the negotiator. The negotiator's efforts at encouraging the perpetrator to ventilate will be aided by negotiator use of open-ended questions, good listening skills and the other interviewing techniques described later in this chapter.

5. **Distraction**
   Attempt to calm the agitated perpetrator by distracting him from the source of his concern.
   At times, an effective means for calming the agitated perpetrator will be to divert his attention temporarily away from the hostage negotiations. This can be done effectively by 1) asking a question totally irrelevant to the hostage situation; 2) asking a question which is relevant to the hostage situation, but opposite to what the perpetrator is likely to express; 3) bringing up a topic of discussion which is irrelevant to the hostage situation; and 4) giving a suggestion which tells the perpetrator to continue doing something that he expects you to want him to stop (or otherwise behave in a manner contrary to his expectancies about negotiators or police).

6. **Nonverbal Cues of Aggression**
   Try to anticipate perpetrator violence by being sensitive to nonverbal cues of aggression.
   You may be able to anticipate likely increases in perpetrator violence by observation of such nonverbal cues as increases in the pace or loudness of his speech, increased restlessness, crouched torso, clenched fists, grinding teeth, dilated pupils, flared nostrils and flushed cheeks.

7. **Avoid Provoking the Perpetrator**
   Avoid any aggressive, offensive or humiliating comments to the perpetrator; do not argue with him; avoid outright rejection of all his demands; avoid sudden surprises.
   All of these provocative actions have the potential, at best, of making your attempts at successful negotiation more difficult and, at worst, of increasing the chances of injury or death for the hostages.

VI. BUILDING RAPPORT

1. **Stall for Time**
   Stall for time.
   Most authorities agree that time works for the police and against the perpetrator. As time progresses, relationships can develop. The development of the perpetrator-negotiator relationship means greater trust, greater likelihood that the negotiator's suggestions will be seriously considered, and greater likelihood of a negotiated surrender of hostages. The development of the perpetrator-hostage relationship means decreased likelihood that the perpetrator will kill or injure the hostages. As time passes, not only relationships develop. The dramatic level of the hostage scene may diminish. Perpetrators get tired, hungry, thirsty and so forth — all opportunities for negotiation of demands that benefit police. Alert negotiators will often be able to take advantage of slips, errors or luck that may occur during protracted negotiations.

2. **Self-Disclosure**
   Disclose information about yourself to the perpetrator, as it may help build rapport.
   People relate more quickly and more positively to others whom they know something about. To help build perpetrator trust in the negotiator, negotiator self-disclosure is encouraged. As it seems appropriate in the conversation (not forced), the negotiator may discuss his own feelings, interests, preferences and even aspects of his professional and personal life. Negotiator self-disclosure, beyond its rapport-building effectiveness, will also prove useful as an information-eliciting technique, i.e., your self-disclosure is often likely to be reciprocated by perpetrator self-disclosure.

3. **Empathy**
   Show high levels of empathy in your response to what the perpetrator says and does.

One of the most effective means for building rapport with the perpetrator is to show him you are able to understand his feelings and thinking, that you are able to step into his shoes for the moment and see the world as he sees it. In being highly empathic, the negotiator need not agree that the situation "really is" as the perpetrator sees it. The important quality of high empathy is that the negotiator communicates his accurate understanding of the perpetrator's view to the perpetrator. Two excellent techniques for communicating high levels of empathy are restatement of content* and reflection of feeling.** In addition, the empathic negotiator will concentrate with intensity on what the perpetrator says and does, will use language that the perpetrator readily understands, and will at times help the perpetrator think through thoughts and feelings that he (the perpetrator) only partly understands.

4. Warmth
Show high levels of warmth in your response to what the perpetrator says and does.

Like empathy, showing high levels of warmth toward the perpetrator is a very effective means of encouraging trust and building rapport. The negotiator can show warmth in a variety of ways: by his tone of voice, his interest, his effort to understand the perpetrator, his concern that they reach a mutual solution, his own commitment to solution finding, and his holding out hope for at least long-term or eventual answers to the perpetrator's demands.

5. Helping Save Face
Help the perpetrator save face.

When the perpetrator feels cornered, publicly defeated or humiliated, he may respond with sudden, violent behavior. If you suspect that such a situation has developed, it will be to your advantage to defuse the situation as rapidly as possible. In addition to the calming procedures described elsewhere in this chapter, you should (1) help the perpetrator retreat gracefully; (2) control the pace of perpetrator concession-giving; (3) provide the perpetrator with relevant, face-saving rationalizations. If appropriate, reassure the perpetrator that you will lead him from the hostage scene in such a manner that it will appear that he was overpowered and arrested by far superior fire-power, rather than having meekly and quietly given up on his own.

---

*See No. 4 in Section VII.

**See No. 5 in Section VII.

6. Don't Belittle Perpetrator
Avoid "talking down" to the perpetrator.

The perpetrator may in a sense be childlike — in his inability to control anger, his bullying use of threats to get what he wants, his emotional ups and downs, and his inability to seek what he wants in more mature and adult ways. But don't treat him like a child. If he feels you are not taking him seriously as an adult, the likelihood of his behaving in a violent manner may increase.

7. Avoid Criticism, Threat and Impatience
Do not criticize, threaten or act impatiently toward the perpetrator.

As noted earlier, time is on **your** side. A problem-solving climate works in **your** favor. If you rush decisions, criticize the perpetrator or threaten him, you are working against your own strategy. You will have ample opportunity to use threats and similar actions if your less directive negotiations fail.

VII. GATHERING INFORMATION

1. Open-Ended Questions
Attempt to gather information from the perpetrator by use of open-ended questions.

Open-ended questions are those which give the perpetrator a chance to give long answers. They are questions which usually begin with "what," "why," or "how." Examples of such questions, as they might occur in a hostage situation, include: "What happened here?", "What do you mean by unfair?", "How do you feel we can compromise?"

2. Closed-Ended Questions
Attempt to gather information from the perpetrator by use of closed-ended questions.

Questions which can be answered with "yes," "no" or a brief, factual reply are closed-ended questions. They usually begin with "do," "is" or "are." Such questions are a valuable part of the negotiator's information-gathering attempt, but must not be overused, particularly as substitutes when open-ended questioning would be more effective. Examples of closed-ended questions include: "Do you accept what I said?", "Is the medicine what you asked for?", "Are you ready to surrender?"

3. Listening
Attempt to gather information from the perpetrator by use of good listening skills.

How well the perpetrator feels the negotiator is listening to him will clearly affect how open and detailed the perpetrator will be. Good listening skills include both things you do and things you avoid doing. The skilled listener makes comments which show the perpetrator that you are interested in what he is saying and are paying attention, e.g., "I see what you mean," or "I can understand that." If safety considerations permit, and the negotiator has gone face-to-face with the perpetrator, the negotiator should also indicate his interest and attention by his gestures, posture and eye contact. The skilled listener tries to avoid conversation with more than one person at a time and reuses calming techniques whenever necessary.

4. Restatement of Content (Paraphrasing)
Attempt to gather information from the perpetrator by use of restatement of content.

Restatement of content consists of saying back to the perpetrator, in words different than his own (i.e., paraphrasing), the essence of what he has already said to you. This information-gathering procedure, like good listening skills, shows your interest, attention and understanding of what the perpetrator is saying and is likely to keep him talking.

5. Reflection of Feeling
Attempt to gather information from the perpetrator by use of reflection of feeling.

Whereas restatement of content emphasizes paraphrasing to the perpetrator one or more of the **facts** in his statement, reflection of feeling focuses on expressing to the perpetrator an understanding of his main **feelings**. To reflect the perpetrator's feelings accurately, the negotiator must pay attention both to what the perpetrator is saying and how he is saying it (its strength, tone, inflection, pace, target, etc.). The main point about reflection of feeling is that when someone feels that you understand his apparent or even somewhat hidden feelings, he is more likely to continue to provide you with information.

6. Discrepancy Confrontation
Attempt to clarify information you receive from the perpetrator by pointing out discrepancies in what he has said.

Discrepancy confrontation means pointing out to the perpetrator discrepancies in either two things he has said (content-content discrepancy), or between something he has said and the way he seems to feel about it (content-feeling discrepancy).

7. **Nature of Demands**
   Expect the perpetrator's demands to be presented to you as:*
   1. Not open to negotiation.
   2. All must be met, and in full.
   3. With a specific time limit.
   4. With a threat of specific consequences if all demands are not met, in full, within the specified time period.

VIII. PERSUADING THE PERPETRATOR

1. **Agree, in Part, with Perpetrator's Views**
   Start your persuasion attempts by agreeing with part of the perpetrator's views.
   Presenting early in your negotiations views which you believe are already held by the perpetrator gives some chance of decreasing part of his resistance to your later arguments.

2. **Deal with Smaller Issues First**
   Try to build a climate of successful negotiation by dealing with smaller, easier to settle items first.
   Dealing first with more easily negotiated items, such as choice of communication channels, food and medicine, will increase the chances that the perpetrator may be open to your views on more central issues, including hostage release. In some hostage situations, this suggestion can best be followed by taking a larger issue and breaking it into several smaller, more workable issues.

3. **State Conclusions**
   Don't just give the perpetrator the facts with the hope that he'll change his mind in your direction.
   Tell him exactly and specifically what conclusions you believe the facts lead to.

4. **Promote Active Listening by the Perpetrator**
   Encourage the perpetrator to actively imagine or "try on" the position you are trying to convince him of.
   Ask him, "What would it be like if . . ?" or similar questions. Passive listening does not promote change in thinking, but active listening by the perpetrator will increase your chances of persuading him.

---

*As the next section of this chapter describes, the suggested negotiator opening response to demands presented in this manner is that the set of demands, as a package, is not acceptable, but we are willing to negotiate some of them.

5. Present Both Sides of the Argument (Yours and His)
Both sides of an issue should be presented by the negotiator.

Presenting your understanding of the perpetrator's side of an argument will help convince him that you are taking him seriously, that you view his argument as having some objective basis, and it will give you the opportunity to try to refute it in comparison to your own views. Anticipating the perpetrator's arguments in this manner will increase your persuasiveness.

6. Consider the Perpetrator's Motivations
Slant your persuasive appeal to the needs and goals of the perpetrator.

Respond to his sense of pride, feelings toward his loved ones, need for status, political views or other of his needs you have learned about or suspect from your background inquiries.

7. Argue against Yourself
Argue against one or more unimportant aspects of your own position.

It will increase your credibility with the perpetrator if you argue against an (unimportant) aspect of your position, impress him with your fairness and open-mindedness, and put the burden on him to yield an aspect of his demands.

8. Point out Similarities
Point out to the perpetrator any perpetrator-negotiator similarities.

People are more persuaded by others they perceive as similar to themselves. Therefore, the negotiator should subtly make sure the perpetrator is aware of negotiator-perpetrator similarities in background, ethnic group, race or other salient characteristics.

9. Request Delayed Compliance
Request delayed compliance.

Especially on issues which you predict will be difficult for the perpetrator to yield on, follow your persuasive attempt with the suggestion that the perpetrator not make up his mind immediately, that he think it over, and, hopefully, accept your view at a later point. A side benefit of requests for delayed compliance are that they add further time to the negotiation process.

10. Minimize Counter Arguments
Minimize counter arguments.

Include in your persuasive attempts weakened versions of the arguments with which the perpetrator is likely to respond. This "co-opts" his response to some extent, and thus may increase the chances he will accept your position.

11. Try to Persuade Gradually
Seek to change the perpetrator's thinking and behavior a small step at a time.

When you try to change too much of the perpetrator's thinking or behavior at one time, a boomerang effect may result. Instead of agreeing with your view, his resistance may **increase.** You are likely to be a more effective negotiator if you attempt piecemeal changes in the perpetrator's thinking.

12. Initiate Issues to Negotiate
Introduce issues into the negotiations yourself so that you can give in on them later as a way of encouraging concessions from the perpetrator.

13. Reward Perpetrator Yielding
Reward the perpetrator for any statements or steps he makes toward successful resolution of the hostage situation.

14. Use of Factual Evidence
Use clear, unambiguous, factual evidence to support your position.

For those items on which you cannot compromise at all, try to provide the perpetrator with clear, unambiguous factual evidence in support of your firmness. The more powerful the evidence you provide, the more likely you will convince the perpetrator that your position will not change.

15. Avoid Audiences
Avoid negotiating in front of others to the extent such "privacy" is possible.

Your negotiating efforts are likely to be less complicated and, perhaps, more successful if audience effects are avoided. Face saving, unexpected pressures or interruptions, over-reaction, increased irrationality, heightened potential for violence are all increased if others can hear (and interfere with) your negotiations. Thus, in a manner consistent with safety concerns, seek to negotiate by direct or telephone communication. Avoid use of bullhorns and similar devices if possible.

16. Avoid Challenging
Do not challenge a perpetrator, or dare him to act.

Leave room for the perpetrator to maneuver. If he feels his back is to the wall, or cornered, there is a good chance he will strike out violently. Maintain the problem-solving climate we have described. Do not threaten the perpetrator, accuse him of bluffing, or otherwise put him on the spot in such a way that he feels he must "save face" by acting violently. If you do so, you may win the debating point but lose your hostages.

17. Reduce Perpetrator Irrationality
Try to decrease the level of perpetrator irrationality.

The perpetrator will often be very anxious, frightened, angry and emotionally unstable. All of these forces may result in irrational thinking patterns, patterns which will make your negotiating attempts more complicated and less likely to succeed. Any steps you can take to reduce perpetrator irrationality will simplify the negotiations, increase their predictability, and make a successful outcome more likely. The several calming procedures we have described elsewhere in this chapter will help decrease perpetrator irrationality. In addition, use suggestion, clarification and concretization to help the perpetrator understand better his own intentions, expected gains and likely costs. When the perpetrator presents issues in a global, intangible, irrational or general manner, recast them in specific, tangible, rational terms.

18. Demands Which Benefit Police
Agree with clear reluctance to any demands which in reality benefit the police position.

There will on occasion be perpetrator demands which, in fact, are of strategic or tactical benefit to the police position, and not the perpetrator's. To obtain "points" as it were, for later barter on yet further issues to benefit the police position, negotiators should yield on these demands with obvious reluctance.

19. Demands Which Benefit Perpetrator
Whenever possible, stall on demands which benefit perpetrator.

We do not want to strengthen the perpetrator's negotiating position. When agreeing to one of his demands would have this effect, e.g., making access to the hostages more difficult, the negotiator's optimal response may be to stall. He should maintain the basic problem-solving climate of the negotiations by clearly showing his willingness to explore (at length) solutions alternative to that being demanded. While striving to avoid angering or increasing the volatility of the perpetrator, the negotiator must if at all possible not yield to situation-worsening perpetrator demands.

20. Offering Suggestions
Offer only those suggestions you feel are clearly necessary, as any

suggestions may speed up the time factor in ways not to your advantage.

21. Keep Perpetrator's Hopes Alive
Keep alive the perpetrator's hope of escape.
The possibility of encouraging acts of desperation through negotiating mistakes must be kept in mind at all times. Such mistakes include any statements which lead the perpetrator to feel he has nothing to lose if he kills his hostages. Through joint problem solving, the perpetrator should be made to believe, he will get some of the results he had in mind when he started the hostage situation. In addition, if at all possible, keep alive his hopes of escape until all hostages have been released.

22. Perpetrator Escape
Be open to the possibility you may have to let the perpetrator escape in trade for hostages.
Your primary responsibility in a hostage incident is the safe release of the hostages. If this can be negotiated along with the perpetrator's surrender, all to the good. If a trade-off, hostages for perpetrator, is the best that can be accomplished, this solution should be accepted. The chance that the perpetrator will be captured later is high. In negotiating such an exchange, however, only accept it if more desirable outcomes have persistently been unobtainable.

8 / A Method for Effective Training: Structured Learning

We have written this chapter for the police **trainer;** that is, the person involved in teaching police officers the hostage situation strategies and tactics presented in the preceding chapters. In chapter seven we examined in considerable detail what skills the effective officer should possess in hostage situations; and, in chapters one through five we provided relevant background information and case examples – information which hopefully can add further to the responding officer's effectiveness. But, before we can maximize officer effectiveness, we must concern ourselves not only with **what** the officer must know, but also with **how** he can best learn it.

An officer could, for example, simply **read** about negotiation procedures. Much of what we all learn comes from "instructional" reading. Thus, trying to learn to conduct effective negotiations by reading about how to do so would certainly succeed to some extent. Or, instead of asking him to read these materials, we could ask him to listen to a series of **lectures** dealing with the same content. As is true with reading as a learning method, we would also expect lectures to result in some gains in knowledge.

But reading and listening to lectures are both passive learning techniques. In both instances the officer takes no action, tries out none of the procedures, practices nothing. For this reason, passive learning approaches often fail to bring about either enduring learning or transfer effects. That is, the officer will tend to forget what he has (passively) learned. Or, even if he does remember much of it, he often will not know how to use or apply this knowledge where it counts – at an actual hostage scene. Thus, a crucial characteristic of the training approach we will recommend in this chapter is that it requires active learning – learning by doing – by the officer-trainee.

But learning by doing is not the only necessary requirement of effective training approaches. After all, much current police training which occurs by "learning on the road" is learning by doing. Such learning via the successes and failures of daily patrol experiences is, however, very inefficient and often dangerous. Certainly, we all learn from experience but it is both a waste of time and effort, and unnecessarily risky, to learn most of what we should know about handling hostage situations by actually trying to handle them. The officer learning this way may have a poor teacher, or worse, he may make an error which results in serious injury, or death to hostages, perpetrator or himself.

Just as the airplane pilot learns by "doing" in a cockpit simulator – in which wasted time is greatly reduced, and real risks to himself and others are essentially eliminated – we would recommend a training approach which also uses simulation. It is, to be sure, less "real" than learning at the scene. But, learning negotiation procedures and related techniques for effective management of hostage situations by having trainees respond to simulated perpetrators and hostages in a classroom has been shown to be a rapid and safe way to teach skills which do endure and do transfer to real-life settings. Thus, the training method we will propose requires active learning by trainees, and involves use of simulation in the form of guided and gradual use of classroom practice and role-playing activities.

Our definition of the officer who is effective in response to a hostage call is one who has learned a variety of behaviors which produce the desired effects on the individuals involved. The effective officer has not only learned this range of safety, information-gathering, calming, rapport-building and persuasion behaviors, but he is flexible enough and skilled enough to be able to use the right behaviors with the right perpetrator at the right time. With these general qualities of effective training in mind, let us now turn to the specific procedures we wish to recommend to those involved in training police officers for effective hostage negotiation.

STRUCTURED LEARNING TRAINING

Structured Learning Training (SLT) consists of four procedures, each of which has been shown to have a substantial and reliable effect on learning. These procedures are modeling, role playing, social reinforcement or other corrective feedback, and transfer training. In each training session, typically involving two trainers and eight to twelve trainees, the trainees are:

1. Played a brief videotape (or shown live "models") depicting the specific skill behaviors that make up effective police action in a hostage situation (modeling).
2. Given substantial opportunity and encouragement to behaviorally rehearse or practice the effective behaviors shown to them by the models (role playing).
3. Provided with corrective feedback, especially in the form of approval or praise, as their role playing of the skill behaviors becomes more and more similar to the tape or live model's behavior (social reinforcement).
4. Asked to participate in all of these procedures in such a way that transfer of the newly learned behaviors from the training setting to real-life hostage negotiations will be highly likely (transfer training).

The specifics of how to use this combination of training procedures in the best manner, to teach negotiation skills, are presented in step-by-step detail in the next chapter. To aid you in understanding and using these procedures most effectively, we will now describe their background and development, as well as other successful uses to which each has been put.

Modeling

Modeling, often also called "imitation" or "observational learning," has been shown time and again to be an effective, reliable and rapid technique both for learning new behaviors or skills, and for strengthening or weakening previously learned behaviors or skills. The variety and sheer number of different behaviors learned, strengthened or weakened due to seeing a model engage in the behavior is quite impressive. Yet, it must be noted that each day most individuals observe dozens and perhaps hundreds of behaviors of others which they do not imitate. In addition to such live models, we read a newspaper and watch television perhaps every day, and see very polished models of purchasing behavior, but do not run out to the store and buy the product. And, in other types of police training, we are often exposed to expensively produced, expertly acted and seemingly persuasive instructional films, but we remain uninstructed. In short, though we are surrounded by all sorts of models engaged in a wide variety of behaviors, we only imitate a very few, and we do so very selectively. To maximize trainee learning, the trainer making use of modeling procedures, as in SLT, is well-advised to be familiar with those characteristics of the model himself, of the way the modeling behavior is shown, and of the trainee, all of which make learning from modeling more likely to occur.

Model characteristics. Greater modeling will occur when the person to be imitated (the model), as compared to the trainee, is:

1. Highly competent or expert.
2. Of high rank or status.
3. Of the same sex.
4. Controls resources desired by the trainee.
5. Friendly and helpful.
6. Rewarded for engaging in the particular behaviors.

Modeling display characteristics. Greater modeling will occur when the taped, filmed or live modeling display shows the model(s) performing the behaviors we want the trainee to imitate:

1. In a vivid and detailed manner.
2. In order from least to most difficult.
3. With considerable repetition.
4. With a minimum of irrelevant details (behavior **not** to be imitated).
5. By use of at least a few different models.

Trainee characteristics. Greater learning by imitation will occur when the trainee:

1. Is instructed to imitate.
2. Is similar to the model in background or attitudes.
3. Likes the model.
4. Is rewarded for engaging in the particular behaviors.

Research on the effectiveness of learning by modeling has been so positive that you may wonder about the necessity for the other components of SLT. If so many different behaviors have been altered successfully by having trainees watch and listen to a model displaying the behaviors, why are role playing, social reinforcement and transfer training necessary?

The answer is clear. Modeling alone is insufficient because, though it yields many positive learning effects, they are very often not enduring effects. The police recruit may watch an experienced officer issue a traffic citation to an angry citizen, and, at that point in time, know how to do so himself. But, if he doesn't participate more actively in the learning process, the trainee is not likely to know how to perform this action effectively for very long. Active participation aids enduring learning.

Structured Learning Training seeks its effectiveness from elements which even go beyond the proven value of active participation. Modeling teaches the trainee **what** to do. To perform what he has observed in an effective and enduring manner, he also needs sufficient practice to know **how** to do it, and sufficient reward to motivate him, or, in effect, tell him **why** he should do it. Modeling shows the **what**, role playing teaches the **how**, social reinforcement provides the **why**. Each alone is not enough; together they offer most of what is necessary for effective and enduring learning. Let us, therefore, turn to the second component of SLT, role playing.

Role Playing

If trainees are to learn how to do something, they must try it. To try many behaviors relevant to effective police functioning under safe conditions, there must be a somewhat "pretend" quality to the tryout. As role playing is used in SLT, this pretend quality is minimized, while a quality of realism is maximized. Officer-trainees do not act out a script prepared for them in advance; but, following the exact skill steps illustrated in the modeling display, they act out the skill behaviors as they think would be most effective and most realistic for them. Thus, in SLT, role playing is not just acting, or psychodrama, or general simulation. It is, instead, behavioral rehearsal – made real for the trainee in every respect possible. This "rehearsal for reality" quality of the use of role playing in SLT, as you will see later in this chapter, increases the chances that what the trainee learns in the training setting will be used in the application setting, i.e., in actual hostage negotiations.

A considerable amount of research has been conducted on the effectiveness of role playing as a training technique. In much of this research, a group of people who share certain attitudes are identified, and then divided into three subgroups. One group, the role players, are then asked to give speeches which take a position **opposite** to their real attitudes. The second group, the listen-only group, hear these speeches but make no speeches of their own. The third group, the control group, neither give nor hear these speeches. Results of these studies show that role players change their attitudes away from their original ones and toward those of the speeches they made, significantly more than either the listen-only or control groups. Role playing has been shown to effectively contribute to attitude change (as well as behavior change) in a wide variety of educational, industrial, clinical and other settings.

As was true for the modeling component of SLT, there are steps you may take to increase the likelihood that role playing will lead to effective learning. Details concerning the use of these "role-play enhancers" are presented in the next chapter; but, in overview here, role playing is more likely to result in trainee learning when the trainee:

1. Feels he has some choice about whether or not to participate in the role playing.
2. Is committed to what role he plays in the sense that he role plays publicly, openly and especially in front of others who know him.
3. Improvises in role playing, rather than following a set script.
4. Is rewarded or reinforced for his role-playing performance.

We pointed out earlier that modeling was a necessary part of effective training, but that modeling alone was not sufficient for enduring learning. Role playing may similarly be viewed as a necessary but insufficient training procedure. After seeing effective police action correctly illustrated (modeling), and trying it himself (role playing), the trainee still needs an answer regarding **why** he should try to learn and use the given negotiation approach. What is his motivation, his incentive, his reward? The trainer's answer to this, we would suggest, is social reinforcement.

Social Reinforcement

Psychologists interested in improving the effectiveness of teaching have drawn an important distinction between acquiring knowledge and actually using it; or, to state it in their words, between **learning** and **performance**. Learning is knowing what to do and how to do it. Performance is actually doing what we have learned. As we said earlier in this chapter, modeling teaches what to do; role playing teaches how to do it. Thus, both modeling and role playing affect learning, not performance. Competent performance (in this case, whether the trainee will actually perform what he has learned in the training center) occurs because of other events - including the reward or reinforcement the trainee receives for his role playing.

In SLT, both the trainers and the other trainees in the group have the responsibility of giving corrective feedback to the trainee who has role played. Most of this feedback involves telling the trainee how well his role-play enactment of the skill's behavioral steps matched the same steps as portrayed by the model on the modeling display. As the trainee's role playing becomes more and more similar to the model's enactment, the feedback increasingly takes the form of approval, praise, compliments and similar social reinforcement. It is this type of feedback which provides the motivation and incentive to continue performing well what the role player has learned.

Just as there are "rules" which, if applied, improve the effectiveness of modeling and role playing, there are a number of research findings which help us improve the effect of social reinforcement on performance. The effect of reinforcement on performance is increased when:

1. There is minimal delay between the completion of the behavior to be reinforced and the delivery of the reinforcement or reward.
2. It is made clear to the trainee which specific behaviors are being reinforced.
3. The nature of the reinforcement being offered is actually perceived as a reward by the trainee.
4. The amount of reinforcement being offered is actually perceived as a reward by the trainee.
5. After making sure the trainee is performing well, the trainer reinforces only some, but not all, performances of the behavior.

At this point in the training sequence, the trainee has learned what to do, practiced how to do it, and been given incentive to perform it well at the training center. What is missing, and what absolutely must be provided, are procedures to increase the chances he will also perform the newly learned skills where they count most, at actual hostage negotiation scenes.

Transfer Training

Transfer training should be a crucial part of any training program. In the training center, away from the pressures of daily patrol, and with the helpful support and encouragement of both the trainers and other trainees, most trainees can learn well and perform competently. It is unfortunate that so many training programs accept competent performance **in the training center** as the criterion for evaluating the success or failure of the program.

While successful trainee performance in the training center is an obvious prerequisite to successful application outside the center, it is very far from a guarantee of it. In fact, more programs fail to transfer than succeed! To maximize the chances that the trainee will be able to transfer his training gains, you are encouraged to reflect the following transfer training principles in your training procedures:

1. **General principles**. Transfer of training is increased by providing the trainee with the general principles, reasons or rules which underlie the procedures and techniques being taught. If the police officer trainee understands **why** certain of his behaviors are likely to lead to certain perpetrator reactions, he is more likely to know how and when to apply these behaviors during actual negotiations.

2. **Response availability**. The more we have practiced something in the past, the more likely we will be able to perform it correctly when necessary. In many training programs, the trainee is required to demonstrate that he can perform a given skill, and once he does so once, the trainer moves on to teaching the next skill. Research on "overlearning" clearly shows that this training strategy is an error. Transfer is increased if trainees are required to perform the correct behaviors not once or twice, but many times. Such repetition may seem unnecessary to some trainees, and they may even complain of boredom, but the correct skills will be more available under the stresses of an actual hostage situation if overlearning has occurred. Thus, you should encourage trainees to repeat correct skill behaviors many times as a training technique.

3. **Identical elements**. The greater the similarity between the training setting and the application setting, the greater the transfer. We may all prefer to go on "retreat" to a comfortable training center when training is to occur, but the more realistic the setting, the better. This may mean that the ideal training context for police officers should contain many of the same physical and interpersonal characteristics as being at a hostage scene. A simulated set-up which is as lifelike as possible should be attempted. The behavior of co-negotiators, back-up personnel, perpetrators, hostages and others in the training setting should resemble their real-life counterparts as much as possible – as should the physical mock-up of the hostage scene.

4. **Performance feedback**. The evaluations and reactions of other people to things we do determine to a great extent whether or not we keep doing them. A trainee may have learned a skill very well in a training center, been socially reinforced by the trainers there, and provided with the transfer-enhancers of general principles, over-

learning and identical elements, but the skills may still fail to transfer to the real world. This failure of transfer can and does occur when the real-life evaluators of our behavior are either indifferent or critical.

Command personnel, the road-wise and experienced partner, and similar highly credible rewarders can make or break a training program. If such respected sources recognize trainee skill behavior with approval, praise or other social reinforcement, the skill behavior will continue to transfer. If the behavior is, instead, either ignored or criticized, it will tend to disappear rapidly. Thus, your training program can get new skill behaviors started, the other three transfer-enhancers can help keep them going, but the feedback trainees get will be especially critical for its continuance.

Research in support of this position is so clear that we urge trainers to maximize positive performance feedback by meeting with command and related personnel, and actually training them in what trainee behaviors to look for and encourage, and in procedures for rewarding the trainee when the behavior is skilled and competent. If command support does not exist, if they are indifferent or opposed to the training effort and this attitude proves to be unchangeable, we firmly recommend that you do not undertake the training effort.

APPLICATIONS OF STRUCTURED LEARNING TRAINING

In this chapter, we have begun to introduce the reader to the four procedures which constitute SLT, and certain means for increasing their effectiveness. This combination of training techniques has been used successfully to teach a wide variety of skills to numerous types of trainees: crisis intervention skills to police officers; management skills to those in industry; social skills to shy and reserved persons; disciplining skills to teachers; empathy skills to parents; helper skills to nurses; self-management skills to patients; and negotiation skills to disputants. In the next chapter we will provide the specific and detailed guidelines for you, the trainer, to use when teaching hostage negotiation skills to police officers.

9 / Structured Learning Manual for Police Trainers

The primary purpose of this chapter is to provide detailed guidelines for effectively conducting Structured Learning Training of police officers in hostage negotiation skills. As we have described in the preceding chapter, structured learning consists of four components, each of which is a well-established training procedure. These procedures are modeling, role playing, social reinforcement and transfer training.

In each training session, a group of eight to twelve trainees are:

1. Played a brief videotape or shown a live demonstration depicting specific skill behaviors shown to be effective in hostage negotiations (modeling).
2. Given extensive opportunity, encouragement and training to behaviorally rehearse, or practice, the effective behaviors they have seen and heard (role playing).
3. Provided corrective feedback and approval or praise as their role playing of the behaviors becomes more and more similar to the tape or live model's behavior (social reinforcement).
4. And, most important, asked to participate in each of these procedures in such a way that transfer of the newly learned behaviors from the training setting to the trainee's real-life setting will be highly likely (transfer training).

Before describing the procedures involved in organizing and actually running structured learning sessions in further detail, we wish to mention briefly what structured learning is **not**. First, it is important to stress that the skill behaviors portrayed by the taped or live model should not be viewed as the one and only way to enact the skill effectively. The goal of Structured Learning Training is to help build a flexible selection of effective negotiating behaviors which the officer can adjust to the demands of the situation. Thus, we urge you to consider the recommended skill behaviors as good examples (as they indeed have been shown to be), but not as the **only** way to effectively perform the skills involved.

A second caution, for those of you using the structured learning modeling tapes, is that these are not instructional tapes in the usual sense. An instructional tape is most typically played to an audience which passively listens to it, and then, at some later date, is supposed to do what was played. Such passive learning is not likely to be enduring learning. Thus, the structured learning modeling tapes should not be played alone, i.e., without role playing and feedback following them. We have demonstrated experimentally that all four components of this training approach are necessary and sufficient for enduring behavior change, and these results should be reflected in the use of these materials and procedures.

Finally, structured learning is not an approach which can be used effectively by all possible trainers. Later in this chapter we will describe in detail the knowledge, skills and sensitivities which a trainer must possess to be effective with this approach.

ORGANIZING THE STRUCTURED LEARNING GROUP

Selection of Trainees*

It is crucial that great care be exercised in choosing officers to participate in hostage negotiator training and, later, in selecting persons to conduct actual negotiations. Desirable and undesirable negotiator characteristics were presented earlier.** These trainee selection criteria are clearly related to negotiation outcome. Almost no amount of training will overcome the deficiencies of a negotiator who, especially under the stress of an actual hostage situation, is too anxious, too aggressive, too unskilled in problem solving, unable to calm the perpetrator or build rapport with him. Select your negotiators with utmost care!

---

*See Appendix A, following this chapter for a recommended battery of psychological tests useful for negotiator selection.
**See "III — The Negotiator," in chapter seven.

For both learning and transfer to occur, each trainee must have ample opportunity to practice what he has seen modeled, receive feedback from other group members and the trainers, and discuss his attempts to apply what he has learned in the training sessions. Yet, each typical session should not exceed three hours in length, since structured learning is intensive, and trainees' efficiency of learning often diminishes beyond this span. A group size of eight to twelve trainees, therefore, is optimal in that it permits the specific training tasks to be accomplished within the allotted time period.

Selection of Trainers

The role-playing and feedback activities which make up most of each structured learning session are a series of "action-reaction" sequences in which effective skill behaviors are first rehearsed (role playing), and then critiqued (feedback). As such, the trainer must both lead and observe. We have found that one trainer is very hard pressed to do both of these tasks well at the same time and, thus, recommend strongly that each session be led by a team of two trainers. Their group leadership skills, interpersonal sensitivity, enthusiasm and a favorable relationship between them are the qualities which appear crucial to the success of training. They must also possess in-depth knowledge of good police procedure, rules and regulations. If they have had considerable negotiator experience, they will be much more credible to the trainees. In addition to these considerations, structured learning trainers must be especially proficient in two types of skills.

The first might best be described as **General Trainer Skills**, i.e., those skills required for success in almost any training effort. These include:
1. Oral communication and group discussion leadership.
2. Flexibility and capacity for resourcefulness.
3. Physical energy.
4. Ability to work under pressure.
5. Empathic ability.
6. Listening skill.
7. Broad knowledge of human behavior.

The second type of requisite skills are **Specific Trainer Skills**, i.e., those relevant to structured learning in particular. These include:
1. In-depth knowledge of structured learning, its background, procedures and goals.
2. How to orient both trainees and supporting staff to structured learning.

3. How to initiate and sustain role playing.
4. Ability to present material in concrete, behavioral form.
5. How to reduce and "turn around" trainee resistance.
6. Procedures for providing corrective feedback.
7. Group management skills, e.g., building cohesiveness, "clique-busting," etc.

For both trainer selection and development purposes, we have found it most desirable to have potential trainers participate, as if they were actual trainees, in a series of structured learning sessions. After this experience, we have had them co-lead a series of sessions with an experienced trainer. In doing so, we have shown them how to conduct such sessions, given them several opportunities to practice what they have seen, and provided them with feedback regarding their performance. In effect, we have used structured learning to teach structured learning.

THE STRUCTURED LEARNING SESSIONS

The Setting

One major principle for encouraging transfer from the training setting to the real-life setting is the rule of identical elements. This rule states that the more similar the two settings (i.e., the greater number of identical physical and social qualities they share), the greater the transfer. We urge you to conduct structured learning in the same general setting as the real-life environment of most participating trainees, and to construct and furnish the training setting to resemble or simulate the likely application setting as much as possible.

You should arrange the training room to make the structured learning procedures easier. A horseshoe layout in which chairs are arranged in the shape of a "U" is one good example of such a helpful arrangement. The officers playing the roles of perpetrator and hostage should be at the front of the room. The trainers should place a chalk board behind and to one side of the role players. Write the specific skill behaviors you're working with at that time on the board so that the officer playing the role of negotiator can see it clearly. As we will note, the trainees who play the role of negotiator in the hostage situation are required to follow and enact the skill's behavioral steps in their role playing. This is a key procedure in structured learning. If possible, other parts of this same room should be furnished (depending on the particular skill being taught) to resemble (at least in rudimentary form) the likely arrangements of people (police, perpetrators, hostages), furniture, barricades and equipment at hostage scenes. In designing the setting, it's also important to keep in mind the trainees' descriptions of where and with whom they think they would have difficulty performing the skills. When no appropriate furniture or materials are available to "set the scene," you can use substitute or even imaginary props.

Open the session by having trainers introduce themselves. Then have each trainee do likewise. Be sure that every trainee has the opportunity to tell the group something about his or her background and training goals. After the initial warm-up period, introduce the program by providing trainees with a brief description of its rationale, training procedures, skill targets and so forth. Typically, in our introduction, we also cover such topics as the importance of skills in working with a very wide variety of hostage situations; the value of skill knowledge and flexibility to the trainee himself; and the manner in which training focuses on altering specific behaviors, and not on attitude change. Next, spend some time discussing these introductory points. After this, you can begin the actual training.

Modeling

The training begins by playing the first modeling tape or enacting the first live demonstration. To ease trainees into structured learning, use tapes or live demonstrations of relatively simple skill behaviors in your first session. Safety skills are often a good example of this. Such content consists of specific skill behaviors which are not difficult to enact for many police officers.

All modeling tapes begin with a narrator setting the scene and stating the tape's behavioral steps. Sets of actors — one or two of whom are in the role the trainees are to adopt during later role playing (negotiator) — portray a series of vignettes in which each skill step is clearly enacted in sequence. The narrator then returns (on the tape), reviews the vignettes, restates the skill steps, and urges their continued use. In our view, this sequence — narrator's introduction, modeling scenes, narrator's summary — constitutes the minimum requirement for a satisfactory modeling tape. In greater detail, we recommend the following format for effective modeling tapes and live demonstrations:

I. **Narrator's Introduction**
1. Introduction of self.
a) Name and title.

b) High status position, e.g., Chief of Police.
2. Introduction of skill.
   a) Name of skill.
   b) General (descriptive) definition.
   c) Operational (skill steps) definition.
3. Incentive statement. How and why skill-presence may be rewarding.
4. Discrimination statement. Examples of skill-absence, and how and why skill-absence may be unrewarding.
5. Repeat statement of skill steps, and request for attention to what follows.

II. Modeling Displays

A number of vignettes of the skill steps being enacted are presented, each vignette portraying the complete set of steps which make up the given skill. A variety of actors (models) and situations are used. Model characteristics (age, sex, etc.) are similar to typical trainee characteristics. Situation characteristics should also reflect common aspects of hostage scenes. The displays portray overt model behaviors, as well as ideational and self-instructional (what one says to oneself) skill steps. Models are provided social reward or reinforcement for enacting the skill. The vignettes are presented in order of increasing complexity.

III. Narrator's Summary

1. Repeat statement of skill steps.
2. Description of rewards to both models and actual trainees for skill usage.
3. Urging of observers to enact the skill steps in the Structured Learning Training session which follows, and, subsequently at actual hostage scenes.

It will often be the case that because of lack of appropriate equipment, materials or personnel, the use of modeling videotapes will not be possible. However, you can still carry out an effective structured learning program to teach hostage negotiation skills. Under these circumstances we recommend that you use live modeling of the skills discussed in this book. Trainers, and experienced officers selected by them, can play the police, perpetrator, hostage and citizen roles which make up each skill demonstration.

It is very important that you carefully prepare each live modeling presentation. Scripts must be carefully planned, thoroughly rehearsed and skillfully enacted before the group. All of the steps which make up a given skill must be clearly portrayed, and in the proper order. The content of each live modeling demonstration must credibly present a hostage situation in a totally realistic manner, or its effectiveness will be minimal. In all, if adequately planned and portrayed, live modeling can be every bit as effective us using videotapes.

The hostage management skills to be modeled are those procedures described in detail in chapter seven. In review, these "Police Procedures for Hostage Negotiation" skills are:

I. Safety
1. Make certain sufficient personnel are both trained in hostage management strategy and tactics and available in adequate numbers for a hostage situation.
2. The hostage management area, inner and outer perimeter personnel, fire power, communications and related resources must be controlled and coordinated by a single source.
3. Influence media, if possible, so no mention is made of tactical plans and resources.
4. Maintain communication among responding personnel.
5. All inner perimeter personnel must be readily identifiable.
6. Negotiator should be physically near the perpetrator, but secure enough that he won't become a hostage himself.
7. Make sure there IS a hostage.
8. Do not fulfill perpetrator requests to bring relatives or friends to the scene.
9. Avoid a show of force, especially when a single perpetrator is involved.
10. Do not negotiate for new weapons, alcohol, narcotics or other items likely to increase the threat to hostage or negotiator safety.
11. If at all possible, avoid movement of the perpetrator and hostages to another location.
12. If it is possible to communicate by any direct means with the hostages, provide them with suggestions designed to increase their safety.

II. Information to Be Obtained
1. Relevant information about the perpetrator should be gathered as completely and rapidly as possible.
2. Relevant information about the hostages should be gathered as completely and rapidly as possible.

3. Relevant information about the hostage site should be gathered as completely and rapidly as possible.

III. **Negotiating Strategies**
1. At the outset, contain and stabilize are your two goals. Avoid all precipitous acts.
2. Establish a problem-solving negotiating climate.
3. Establish a compromising climate.
4. Avoid use of a forcing negotiating strategy.
5. Avoid use of a soft-bargainer negotiating strategy.
6. Use the negotiating strategy which your prenegotiation investigation reveals best fits the nature of the perpetrator involved.
7. Use of force should be planned for, but implemented only as a last resort.

IV. **Calming the Perpetrator**
1. Attempt to calm the agitated perpetrator by showing understanding of his feelings.
2. Attempt to calm the agitated perpetrator by displaying your own calmness to him.
3. Attempt to calm the agitated perpetrator by reassuring him.
4. Attempt to calm the agitated perpetrator by encouraging him to talk.
5. Attempt to calm the agitated perpetrator by distracting him from the source of his concern.
6. Try to anticipate perpetrator violence by being sensitive to non-verbal cues of aggression.
7. Avoid any aggressive, offensive or humiliating comments to the perpetrator; do not argue with him; avoid outright rejection of all his demands; avoid sudden surprises.

V. **Building Rapport**
1. Stall for time.
2. Disclose information about yourself to the perpetrator, as it may help build rapport.
3. Show high levels of empathy in your response to what the perpetrator says and does.
4. Show high levels of warmth in your response to what the perpetrator says and does.
5. Help the perpetrator save face.
6. Avoid "talking down" to the perpetrator.

    7. Do not criticize, threaten or act impatiently toward the perpetrator.

VI. Gathering Information

1. Attempt to gather information about the perpetrator by use of open-ended questions.
2. Attempt to gather information from the perpetrator by use of closed-ended questions.
3. Attempt to gather information from the perpetrator by use of good listening skills.
4. Attempt to gather information from the perpetrator by use of restatement of content.
5. Attempt to gather information from the perpetrator by use of reflection of feeling.
6. Attempt to clarify information you receive from the perpetrator by pointing out discrepancies in what he has said.
7. Expect the perpetrator's demands to be presented to you with a threat of specific consequences if all demands are not met, in full, within a specific time period.

VII. Persuading the Perpetrator

1. Start your persuasion attempts by agreeing with part of the perpetrator's views.
2. Try to build a climate of successful negotiation by dealing with smaller, easier-to-settle items first.
3. Don't just give the perpetrator the facts with the hope that he'll change his mind in your direction; draw conclusions from these facts for him.
4. Encourage the perpetrator to actively imagine or "try on" the position you are trying to convince him of.
5. Present both sides of the argument (yours and his).
6. Consider the perpetrator's motivations.
7. Argue against one or more unimportant aspects of your own position.
8. Point out to the perpetrator any perpetrator-negotiator similarities.
9. Request delayed compliance.
10. Minimize counter-arguments.
11. Seek to change the perpetrator's thinking and behavior a small step at a time.
12. Introduce issues into the negotiations yourself so that you can give in to them later as a way of encouraging concessions from the perpetrator.

13. Reward the perpetrator for any statements or steps he makes toward successful resolution of the hostage situation.
14. Use clear, unambiguous, factual evidence to support your position.
15. Avoid negotiating in front of others to the extent such "privacy" is possible.
16. Do not challenge a perpetrator, or dare him to act.
17. Try to decrease the level of perpetrator irrationality.
18. Agree with clear reluctance to any demands which in reality benefit the police position.
19. Whenever possible, stall on demands which benefit perpetrator.
20. Offer only those suggestions you feel are clearly necessary, as any suggestions may speed up the time factor in ways not to your advantage.
21. Keep alive the perpetrator's hope of escape.
22. Be open to the possibility you may have to let perpetrator escape in trade for hostages.

Role Playing

A spontaneous discussion will almost invariably follow the playing of a modeling tape or the live demonstration of a skill. Trainees will comment on the skill steps, the actors, and very often, on how the situation or skill problem shown might occur in their own work. At this point in time, you should divide the trainees into groups of two to four trainees each, and instruct them to prepare for role playing. This preparation is designed to make the role playing, which follows viewing of the modeling tapes or the live demonstration as realistic as possible.

The purpose of structured learning is not practice of exercises handed down by someone else, not rehandling old hostage calls but, instead, **behavioral rehearsal**; that is, practice for hostage situations which the trainee is actually likely to face. Each group of four trainees is instructed to develop a hostage event [planning the specific roles of perpetrator(s), hostage(s), relatives or other citizens], and enact this event as realistically as possible to two other officer-trainees who have been instructed to deal with the call by following the skill illustrated on the modeling tapes or live demonstrations. The specific instructions you give to the trainees preparing the hostage enactment follow.

Role-Playing Instructions

Your task during this preparation period will be to design a skit in which a hostage situation occurs. Afterwards, the skit will be performed with members of your group portraying the perpetrator, hostage and other citizens involved, while one or more members of another group portray a police officer intervening in that situation. All other trainees will then participate in the critique which follows the skit.

The skit will require careful preparation for effectiveness as a learning/teaching method. We suggest you cover the following steps:

1. Talk about hostage cases you've known or can imagine; select one that can be effectively portrayed, and that promises to be a good learning vehicle for the audience.
2. Discuss the personalities and situations involved.
3. Select group members to portray the roles.
4. Help the actors become familiar with their roles, with what they will say and do before the "police" arrive.
5. Help the actors practice and become "natural" in their roles. Discourage overacting. It is **essential** that after the police arrive, your actors react naturally to what the "police" do, and not according to some script. Remember, when your skit is presented, after the intervening officer(s) arrive, the actors should respond to the officer(s) as they think their characters would respond.

As noted earlier, two other trainees are chosen to serve as the responding officers. Their task is to handle the situation effectively, by using the several negotiating skills which have been demonstrated. All other trainees in the larger group serve as observers, whose later feedback is designed to be of use to the two responding officers.

Before the given role play actually begins, you should deliver the following instructions:

1. To the two trainees responding to the call (negotiators): In responding to the call you are about to hear, follow and enact the relevant skill steps. Do not leave any out, and follow them in the proper sequence.

2. To the trainees enacting the hostage situation (perpetrator, hostage): React as naturally as possible to the behavior of the responding officers. Within the one limitation of not endangering anyone's physical safety, it is important that your reactions to the responding officers be as real-life as possible.

3. To all other trainees (observers): Carefully observe how well the responding officers follow the skill steps, and take notes on this for later discussion and feedback.

One of the trainers then instructs the role players to begin. It is your main responsibility at this point to be sure negotiators keep role playing, and that they try to follow the skill steps while doing so. If they "break role," and begin making comments or explaining background events, etc., you should firmly instruct them to resume their roles. One trainer should position himself near the chalkboard and point to each step in turn, as the role play unfolds, being sure none is missed or enacted out of order. If either responder feels the role play is not progressing well and wishes to start it over, this is appropriate. Do not permit interruptions of any kind from the group until the role play is completed.

The role playing should be continued until all the skits have been presented and all trainees (negotiators) have had an opportunity to participate, even if the same skill must be carried over to a second or third session. Note that while the skill steps of each role play in the series remain the same, the actual content should change from role play to role play. It is hostage situations as they actually occur, or could occur, which should be the content of the given role play. When completed, each trainee should be better armed to act appropriately in the given reality situations.

We would like to point out a few further procedural matters relevant to role playing, as each will serve to increase its effectiveness. Role reversal is often a useful role-play procedure. An officer role playing a hostage problem may have a difficult time perceiving the perpetrator's viewpoint, and vice versa. Having them exchange roles and resume the role playing can be most helpful in this regard.

At times, it may be worthwhile for the trainer to assume the perpetrator role, in an effort to expose trainees to the handling of types of reactions not otherwise role played during the session. It is here that your flexibility and creativity will certainly be called upon. Finally, role playing at times may become **too** realistic and the possibility of physical injury to one of the participants may appear likely. You should plan some means for getting trainee attention quickly in the event that it becomes necessary to stop the role playing immediately.

Corrective Feedback/Social Reinforcement

After completing each role play, you should have a brief feedback period. The goals of this activity are to let the responders know how well they "stayed with" the skill steps, or in what ways they departed from them. It also lets them know the psychological impact of their enactment on the perpetrators, and encourages them to try out effective role-play behaviors in real life. To implement this feedback process, we suggest you follow a sequence of eliciting comments from:

1. **The role-play perpetrator**, i.e., "How did the negotiating officers make you feel?" "What are you likely to do now?"
2. **The observing trainees**, i.e., "How well were the skill steps followed?" "What **specific** behaviors did you like or dislike?"
3. **The trainers**, who comment, in particular, on how well the steps were followed, and who provide social reinforcement (praise, approval, encouragement) for close following. To be most effective, reinforcement provided by the trainers should be offered in accordance with the following rules:

a) Provide reinforcement **immediately** after role plays which follow the skill steps.
b) Provide reinforcement **only** after role plays which follow the skill steps.
c) Vary the specific content of the reinforcements offered.
d) Provide enough role-playing activity for each group member to have sufficient opportunity to be reinforced.
e) Provide reinforcement in an amount consistent with the quality of the given role play.
f) Provide no reinforcement when the role play departs significantly from the skill steps. (except for "trying" in the first session or two).
g) In later sessions, space out the reinforcement you provide so that not every good role play is reinforced.

4. **The role-play responders themselves**, who comment on their own enactment and on the comments of others.

In all these critiques, it is crucial that you maintain the behavioral focus of structured learning. Comments must point to the presence or absence of specific, concrete behaviors, and not take the form of general evaluative comments or broad generalities. Feedback, of course, may be positive or negative in content. At minimum, you can praise a "poor" performance (major departures from the skill steps) as a "good try" at the same time you criticize its real faults.

If at all possible you should give trainees who fail to follow the relevant skill steps in their role play the opportunity to re-role play these same steps after they've received corrective feedback. At times, as a further feedback procedure, we have audiotaped or videotaped entire role plays. The "actors" are often too busy "doing" to reflect on their own behavior. Giving them later opportunities to observe themselves on tape can be an effective aid to learning.

Since a prime goal of structured learning is skill flexibility, a role-play trainee who departs markedly from the skill steps may not necessarily be "wrong." That is, what he does may, in fact, "work" in some situations. Trainers should stress that it is an effective "**alternative**" they are trying to teach, and that the trainee would do well to have it in his repertoire (collection) of skill behaviors — available to use when it is appropriate.

As a final feedback step, after all role playing and discussion of it are completed, you should replay the modeling tape, or repeat the live demonstration of the particular skill. This step, in a sense, summarizes the session and leaves trainees with a final overview of effective negotiating skills.

Transfer Training

The prime purpose of several aspects of the training sessions described above is to enhance the likelihood that learning in the training setting will transfer to the trainee's actual work environment. Making sure that the trainees in the perpetrator role create a hostage event which is as realistic as possible (both in terms of their own behavior and the physical setting and props of the role play) is one example of an aid to transfer.

Another is to try to have the two trainees who are in the responder role for a given skit, be two officers who actually work together on the road. Sheer practice is another means which increases the chances that what the officers learn in training will be used in the community. Such practice of a skill occurs by not only serving as a responder, but also when the trainee serves as either a perpetrator or an observer.

Transfer of training is also a function of the trainee's motivation. "Learning" concerns the question: **Can** he do it? "Performance" is a matter of: **Will** he do it? Trainees will perform as trained if, and only if, they have genuine and active environmental support. Stated simply, new behaviors persist if they are rewarded; diminish if they are ignored or actively challenged. Obviously, therefore, you should not undertake a structured learning program (or any training program) unless you can realistically expect some appreciable level of environmental support from your command and other supervisory personnel.

Resistance and Resistance Reduction

As happens in all training approaches, a minority of the trainees who take part in structured learning may be resistive. In one or more of a variety of ways, they may seek to block or avoid trainer efforts to conduct the session as we have defined it throughout this chapter. They may argue about the accuracy or relevance of the content of the modeling tape or live demonstration; they may claim that the absence of danger during role playing makes it so different from real life that it is useless; they may show boredom, disinterest and unconcern. In all, we have identified 15 different ways in which resistance may occur. We have listed the types of resistance in Table 9.1, and briefly mentioned the general approaches to reducing such resistance which we have found useful. In Table 9.2, we have more fully identified several means for dealing effectively with trainee resistance.

Table 9.1.
Types of Trainee Resistance

I. **Active Resistance to Participation**
    1. Participation, but not as instructed
    2. Refusal to role play
    3. Lateness
    4. Cutting
    Reduce this resistance by: a) encouraging empathically, b) reducing threat, c) instructing.

II. **Inappropriate Behavior**
    1. Can't remember
    2. Inattention
    3. Excessive restlessness
    Reduce this resistance by: a) simplifying, b) terminating responses, c) instructing.

III. **Inactivity**
    1. Apathy
    2. Minimal participation
    3. Minimal ability to understand
    Reduce this resistance by: a) reducing threat, b) eliciting responses, c) instructing.

IV. **Hyperactivity**
    1. Interrupts

2. Monopolizes
3. Trainer's helper
4. Jumping out of role
5. Disagrees
Reduce this resistance by: a) encouraging empathically, b) terminating responses, c) reducing threat.

Table 9.2.
Methods for Reducing Trainee Resistance

I.   Simplification Methods
1. Reinforce minimal trainee accomplishment.
2. Shorten the role play.
3. Have the trainee read a script portraying the learning points.
4. Have the trainee play a passive role (or even a nonspeaking role) in role playing.

II.   Threat Reduction Methods
1. Use live modeling of negotiator role by the trainer.
2. Reassure trainee.
3. Clarify any aspects of the trainee's task which are still unclear.

III. Elicitation of Responses Methods
1. Call for volunteers.
2. Introduce topics for discussion.
3. Ask specific trainee to participate, preferably choosing someone who has made eye contact with the leader.

IV.   Termination of Responses Methods
1. Interrupt ongoing behavior.
2. Extinguish through inattention to trainee behavior.
3. Back off contact and get others to participate.
4. Urge trainee to get back on correct track.

V.   Instruction Methods
1. Coach and prompt.
2. Instruct in specific procedures and applications.

VI.   Empathic Encouragement Method (Six Steps)
1. Offer the resistant trainee the opportunity to explain in greater detail his reluctance to role play, and listen nondefensively.
2. Clearly express your understanding of the resistant trainee's feelings.

3. If appropriate, respond that the trainee's view is a viable alternative.
4. Present your own view in greater detail with both supporting reasons and probable outcomes.
5. Express the appropriateness of delaying a resolution of the trainer-trainee difference.
6. Urge the trainee to tentatively try to role play the given learning points.

This consideration of trainee resistance and its management completes our presentation of the methods and purposes of the structured learning approach to training effective negotiators. Hostage situations are dangerous, complex and difficult to resolve. Their successful management requires very high levels of the full range of negotiation skills described in this book. We close with the sincere hope that our presentation will contribute in significant ways to the learning of such skills and thus to the rapid and successful resolution of actual hostage situations.

Appendix A
Negotiator Selection

As part of their Counter Terrorism and Hostage Program, the New York State Police requested Dr. Miron to bring together and construct a series of psychological tests which would form an effective test battery for purposes of selecting skilled hostage negotiators. The *Negotiator Selection Instrument* was the product of this effort. This is a seven-test battery, requiring approximately four hours to complete, and consisting of the following tests:

1. *Background Information Form.* This form requests information from the applicant regarding his personal background, emergency data, experience record, military service, education, language skills, special physical abilities, courses or training received, personal weapons and weapons skills.

2. *Motivation Analysis Test (MAT).* This instrument, developed by the Institute for Personality and Ability Testing under the direction of Dr. Raymond Cattell is designed to assess a person's interests, drives and the strengths of his value systems. Unlike personality inventories, it measures those aspects of an individual's motivations which can be expected to form the immediate and longer-term basis of his goals and aspirations. The test is the result of an extensive research program of empirical studies and has been used in a number of applied settings in which it is important to gauge an individual's motivations for seeking a particular position or assignment. The test is scored along 10 basic dimensions as follows:

Title	Brief Description
Mating	Amount of the normal, heterosexual mating drive.
Assertiveness	Strength of the drive for self-assertion, and achievement.
Fear	Degree of alertness to external danger.
Narcism-Comfort	Level of drive for self-indulgence and comfort.
Pugnacity-Sadism	Degree of destructive or hostile impulses.
Self-Concept	Degree of concern about social repute, the self and delayed rewards.
Superego	Strength of conscience.
Career Sentiments	Interest in career goals.
Sweetheart-Spouse Sentiment	Degree of attachment to spouse or sweetheart.
Home-Parental Sentiment	Attitudes regarding traditions of home and parents.

Normative scores for each of these dimensions are provided by the test-makers for a variety of different adult populations for comparison with individual test scores. The illustration in Figure A.1 depicts the average scores of 32 New York State Police special weapons team members.

The reader will observe that these men, for the most part, fall within the boundaries of the average scores obtained from the general adult population. They differ from the ordinary population with respect to the strengths of their assertiveness, pugnacity, superego and comfort characteristics. For this group of individuals, departure from the general population on these dimensions is not to be considered either abnormal or undesirable. Higher than average pugnacity is an essen-

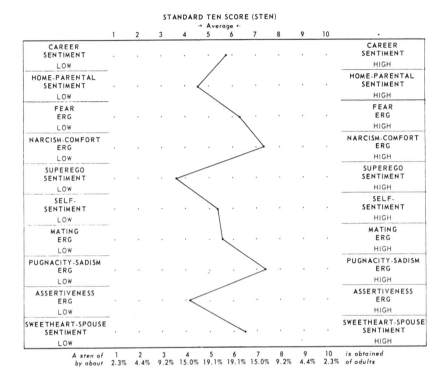

Figure A1: MAT (Motivation Analysis Test) Dynamic Structure Profile for 32 New York State Police Shooters. (Source: Motivation Analysis Test Copyright © 1961, 1964, The Institute for Personality and Ability Testing, 1602 Coronado Drive, Champaign, Illinois, USA. All rights reserved. Printed in USA. Reproduced by permission of the copyright owner.

140   *Hostage*

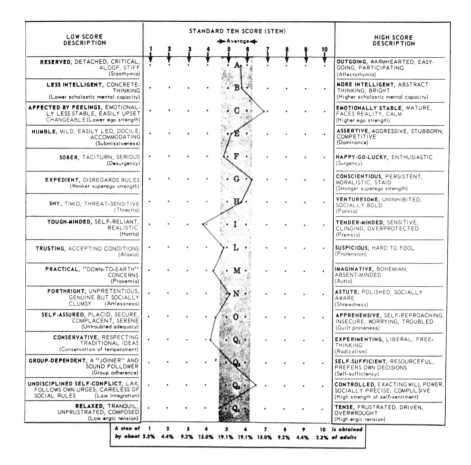

LOW SCORE DESCRIPTION	STANDARD TEN SCORE (STEN) Average	HIGH SCORE DESCRIPTION
RESERVED, DETACHED, CRITICAL, ALOOF, STIFF (Sizothymia)	A	OUTGOING, WARMHEARTED, EASY-GOING, PARTICIPATING (Affectothymia)
LESS INTELLIGENT, CONCRETE-THINKING (Lower scholastic mental capacity)	B	MORE INTELLIGENT, ABSTRACT-THINKING, BRIGHT (Higher scholastic mental capacity)
AFFECTED BY FEELINGS, EMOTIONAL-LY LESS STABLE, EASILY UPSET CHANGEABLE (Lower ego strength)	C	EMOTIONALLY STABLE, MATURE, FACES REALITY, CALM (Higher ego strength)
HUMBLE, MILD, EASILY LED, DOCILE, ACCOMMODATING (Submissiveness)	E	ASSERTIVE, AGGRESSIVE, STUBBORN, COMPETITIVE (Dominance)
SOBER, TACITURN, SERIOUS (Desurgency)	F	HAPPY-GO-LUCKY, ENTHUSIASTIC (Surgency)
EXPEDIENT, DISREGARDS RULES (Weaker superego strength)	G	CONSCIENTIOUS, PERSISTENT, MORALISTIC, STAID (Stronger superego strength)
SHY, TIMID, THREAT-SENSITIVE (Threctia)	H	VENTURESOME, UNINHIBITED, SOCIALLY BOLD (Parmia)
TOUGH-MINDED, SELF-RELIANT, REALISTIC (Harria)	I	TENDER-MINDED, SENSITIVE, CLINGING, OVERPROTECTED (Premsia)
TRUSTING, ACCEPTING CONDITIONS (Alaxia)	L	SUSPICIOUS, HARD TO FOOL (Protension)
PRACTICAL, "DOWN-TO-EARTH" CONCERNS (Praxernia)	M	IMAGINATIVE, BOHEMIAN, ABSENT-MINDED (Autia)
FORTHRIGHT, UNPRETENTIOUS, GENUINE BUT SOCIALLY CLUMSY (Artlessness)	N	ASTUTE, POLISHED, SOCIALLY AWARE (Shrewdness)
SELF-ASSURED, PLACID, SECURE, COMPLACENT, SERENE (Untroubled adequacy)	O	APPREHENSIVE, SELF-REPROACHING, INSECURE, WORRYING, TROUBLED (Guilt proneness)
CONSERVATIVE, RESPECTING TRADITIONAL IDEAS (Conservatism of temperament)	Q1	EXPERIMENTING, LIBERAL, FREE-THINKING (Radicalism)
GROUP-DEPENDENT, A "JOINER" AND SOUND FOLLOWER (Group adherence)	Q2	SELF-SUFFICIENT, RESOURCEFUL, PREFERS OWN DECISIONS (Self-sufficiency)
UNDISCIPLINED SELF-CONFLICT, LAX, FOLLOWS OWN URGES, CARELESS OF SOCIAL RULES (Low integration)	Q3	CONTROLLED, EXACTING WILL POWER, SOCIALLY PRECISE, COMPULSIVE (High strength of self-sentiment)
RELAXED, TRANQUIL, UNFRUSTRATED, COMPOSED (Low ergic tension)	Q4	TENSE, FRUSTRATED, DRIVEN, OVERWROUGHT (High ergic tension)

A sten of 1 2 3 4 5 6 7 8 9 10 is obtained by about 2.3% 4.4% 9.2% 15.0% 19.1% 19.1% 15.0% 9.2% 4.4% 2.3% of adults

Figure A2: 16 PF Test Profile for 32 New York State Police Shooters. (Source: Copyright © 1956, 1973, Institute for Personality and Ability Testing, 1602 Coronado Drive, Champaign, Illinois, USA. All property rights reserved. Printed in USA. Reproduced by permission of the copyright owner.

tial trait for one who may be expected to have to use his marksman skills. Lowered assertiveness is similarly desirable in one who will be expected to function as a team member under the orders of a commanding officer. The generally lowered superego responses also reflect the desirable quality of **not** being so conscience stricken so as not to be able to take action when called upon. The average scores on this dimension are not so low as to provide concern that these men do not value moral principles; to the contrary they reflect an effective approach to the difficult task they must perform. The slightly higher than average scores of this group on the "Narcism-Comfort" dimension undoubtedly reflect one of the motivations for volunteering for the special training, i.e., in part as avoidance of the more routine aspects of usual police work. Such motivation is to be expected and is not cause for concern.

This profile of motivation is presented to point up what we believe should be the differing motivations for those who might make effective negotiators. Shooters should differ from negotiators in a number of ways. A shooter at some point must be capable of the most extreme aggressive response of police work. A negotiator, on the other hand, for much of his work needs to be willing to submerge both self and aggressiveness in his attempts to negotiate a nonviolent solution to a crisis. Ideally, the negotiator candidate probably should display somewhat lower than average scores on the dimensions of "Assertiveness," "Pugnacity-Sadism" and "Self," and somewhat higher scores on the "Fear" dimension. Remember that we are talking about specific motivational test scores and not about personality characteristics. For example, higher scores on the "Fear" dimension do not reflect anxiety or fearfulness, they are instead to be interpreted as alertness and responsiveness to external dangers obviously vital in one who must be able to respond to subtle cues of potential danger in a crisis situation.

3. *The 16 Personality Factor Questionnaire (16PF).* This instrument, also developed by Dr. Cattell and his coworkers at the Illinois Institute, is a widely used test of personality. The dimensions of personality measured on this test represent a well-accepted theoretical basis for assessing individual variations in those relatively enduring characteristics which distinguish one individual from another. The 16 dimensions of the instrument and their descriptions along with the average profiles for the 32 New York State Police Shooters are provided in Figure A.2.

Notice that these men tend to be more emotionally stable, tough-minded, conservative and controlled than the average population of adults. They are also more practical and self-assured. These are clearly highly desirable traits on which to differ from others in view of the nature of their work. In all regards, this profile reflects the best attributes of the professional policeman. Indeed, these traits are also those one would ideally want in a negotiator.

Taken together and properly interpreted by one trained in their use, these two instruments can be expected to contribute much toward an accurate picture of the characteristics of those who can be expected to be most successful in their assignments. Both of these copyrighted tests may be obtained from the Institute for Personality and Ability Testing, 1602 Coronado Drive, Champaign, Illinois, at a nominal fee. The Institute also offers a scoring and interpretation service which will provide analyses of individual test results.

4. *Pictured Situations Test (PST).* Since there are problems which are peculiar to the training of negotiation skills, it was felt that some test was required that might assess a negotiator training candidate's preconceptions and attitudes regarding specific issues in negotiation. To meet this need, the New York State Police training staff under the direction of Walter Hornberger and Dr. Miron collaborated in the development of a series of cartoon-like depictions of situations a negotiator might have to confront. In each situation, the candidate is asked to place himself in the role of the pictured person and provide a verbal response which he feels would be most appropriate. There are, of course, no right or wrong answers to such a test. But an analysis of the character of the test-taker's responses can give a good indication of the general character of how he thinks about the depicted aspects of his work. Additionally, the test can be used to identify preconceptions which need to be specifically addressed in training, both as general considerations and as individualized problems. The test is reprinted herein (see Subtest C) with the permission of the New York State Police and the Special Hostage Training Staff headed by Walter Hornberger, Ely Probst and James O'Toole.

5. *Belief Alternatives Test.* This instrument was developed by J. B. Rotter as a research tool designed to measure the degree to which an individual perceives his rewards to be the consequences of internal, i.e., personally controlled or external, e.g., chance or uncontrollable, forces. If the individual tends to believe that the outcomes of his actions are determined by chance, fate or some other external force which he has minimal control over, that person Rotter identifies as one

exhibiting perceptions of external locus of control. If the individual perceives the outcomes of his behavior to be under his personal control, determined by his own abilities and personality rather than by outside forces, he is said to be internally controlled. Originally published as a monograph in 1966 (Rotter, J. B. Generalized expectancies for internal versus external control of reinforcement. *Psychological Monographs,* 1966, *80,* 609), the test has since been extensively employed in a number of different applications.

As a tool for selection of potential negotiators, it is used by the New York State Police to identify those candidates who may be extreme in either "internal" or "external" qualities. We believe that the most effective negotiator should be one who believes that the outcomes of his negotiation are only minimally affected by forces outside of his control. Rather than feeling that chance or fate will dictate the resolution of the crisis, the effective negotiator must believe that the outcome can be controlled by his actions and skills.

6. *Personal Opinion Test.* This instrument is designed to assess the degree and nature of the personal opinions held by the candidate which may reflect rigidity or dogmatism regarding certain issues. For example, if a candidate strongly agrees with the assertion that "most people just don't know what's good for them" or "it's better to be a dead hero than a live coward" he or she is unlikely to be very effective as a negotiator. The items for the test as employed in the New York State Police selection instrument are drawn from the research literature on rigidity and dogmatism. Many of these test items can be found in M. Rokeach's monograph entitled "Political and Religious Dogmatism: An Alternative to the Authoritarian Personality." *Psychological Monographs,* 1956, *70,* 425.

7. *Characteristic Qualities Test.* This instrument developed specifically for the New York State Police, is designed to assess the candidate's perceptions of the qualities he feels best describe the average hostage, hostage-taker and negotiator. For each of these types of persons, the candidate is given a checklist of 120 qualities. He is asked to indicate the degree to which he believes each of these qualities describes the three kinds of persons. From the pattern of responses, it is possible to obtain a detailed picture of the preconceptions and biases each candidate brings to his training as a negotiator. If an individual, for example, were to feel that hostages in general, were best described by the qualities **stupid, simpleminded** and **weak**, it is clear that such preconceptions might seriously affect how such an individual might attempt to negotiate. Consequently, both the indi-

vidual trainees and the group of trainees should be given back their responses to this test and the information used as specific teaching points which should be either reinforced as accurate generalizations or changed as inaccurate.

A copy of the *Negotiator Selection Instrument* just described appears on the following pages. For those parts of the instrument held in copyright (Subtests A, B, D, E) by others, we have provided information indicating where the interested reader may obtain a copy. Those tests which are held in copyright by the New York State Police or by Dr. Miron appear in full. For further information about the use of the *Negotiator Selection Instrument,* please contact Dr. Miron or T/Sgt. W. Hornberger, Albany Campus, New York State Police.

NEGOCIATOR SELECTION INSTRUMENT
Instructions

This booklet contains test materials designed to determine personal differences in potential negotiator selectees. The test results will be used to indicate the characteristics of successful and effective negotiators. For most of these tests there are no right or wrong answers, it is the nature of your personal opinions and beliefs we are interested in. As an officer designated by your commander as one who might make an effective negotiator, your answers to these tests will help us to assess your distinctive qualities. The test booklet is composed of the following subparts:

1. *Background Information Form*
2. *MAT Test* (Subtest A)
3. *16PF* (Subtest B)
4. *Pictured Situations Test* (Subtest C)
5. *Belief Alternatives* (Subtest D)
6. *Personal Opinion Test* (Subtest E)
7. *Characteristic Quality Test* (Subtest F)
   A. *Hostage*
   B. *Hostage-taker*
   C. *Negotiator*

Each subpart is preceded by instructions for that part. The total test should take approximately 4 to 5 hours to complete. Do each test in the order in which it appears in your booklet. You may complete each test at separate times but be sure to complete any one of the tests at the same sitting. Mail your completed test booklets to Albany Headquarters in the enclosed envelope.

> Attach four (4) recent
> photos (last 60 days)

APPLICATION
COUNTER TERRORIST/HOSTAGE NEGOTIATION
TRAINING PROGRAM

PERSONAL DATA   Date _____

NAME _____ SEX _____
        (LAST)   (FIRST)   (MI)

DEPARTMENT _____

RANK _____ TIME AT PRESENT RANK _____

RESIDENCE _____
                              (STREET)

_____
   (CITY - VILLAGE - TOWN)   (COUNTY)   (STATE)   (ZIP CODE)

HOME PHONE _____ _____
              (AREA CODE)   (NUMBER)

MARITAL STATUS: MARRIED (   )   WIFE'S NAME _____

   NUMBER OF CHILDREN _____   SINGLE ( )   SEPARATED ( )
                                   DIVORCED ( )   WIDOWED ( )

HEIGHT _____ WEIGHT _____ DOB _____

EMERGENCY DATA

NEXT OF KIN TO BE NOTIFIED _____

ADDRESS _____

TELEPHONE NUMBER _____ RELATIONSHIP _____

RELIGION _____ BLOOD TYPE _____

SPECIAL MEDICAL CONSIDERATIONS E.G. ALLERGIES TO ANTIBIOTICS,
HIGH BLOOD PRESSURE, ETC. -
YES _____ NO _____ IF YES, INDICATE _____

_____

_____

DO YOU SMOKE: YES ( )   NO ( )

EXPERIENCE RECORD

CURRENT DUTY ASSIGNMENT (Explain briefly) _____

_____

IMMEDIATE SUPERIOR _____
                            (RANK)   (NAME)

TELEPHONE NUMBER _____   _____
                        (AREA CODE)   (NUMBER)

PREVIOUS DUTY ASSIGNMENTS
AND SERVICE TIME:

DUTY ASSIGNMENT	RANK	FROM	TO

MILITARY SERVICE

DUTY ASSIGNMENT	RANK	FROM	TO

EDUCATION

A) HIGHEST LEVEL (Circle One) 1 — 2 — 3 — 4 — 5 — 6 — 7 — 8 — 9 — 10 — 11 — 12
    COLLEGE 1 — 2 — 3 — 4 yrs. (Circle)
    TYPE DEGREE _____

B) OTHER DEGREE(S) OBTAINED (Indicate degree and college) _____

_____

LANGUAGE ARTS

LANGUAGE _____   SPOKEN FLUENTLY_____ _____
                                                   (YES)   (NO)

READ_____WRITE _____ WHERE

LEARNED _____

OTHER ABILITIES OR EXPERTISE, SUCH AS LEARNED FROM PAST EMPLOYMENT OR HOBBIES: _____

_____

_____

_____

SPECIAL PHYSICAL ABILITIES (Boxing, Karate, Judo, etc.) (Indicate) _____

_____

_____

COURSES OR TRAINING RECEIVED

PROGRAMS _____

WHEN _____ WHERE _____

AWARD/CERTIFICATE _____

DRIVER'S LICENSE # _____ TYPE LICENSE _____

YEARS DRIVING _____

MILEAGE PER YEAR _____

PERSONAL WEAPONS (Type, owned — include rifles, shotguns, etc.) (Indicate expertise)

_____

_____

_____

Any special shooting designation (expert — instructor — etc.) _____

_____

_____

_____

_____

_____

Briefly give your opinion about the Counter Terrorist/Hostage Training Program and use of unarmed negotiators:

_____

_____

_____

_____

_____

Briefly describe your particular ethnic background and why you feel it may be an advantage as a negotiator:

_____

_____

_____

_____

_____

SUBTEST A
MAT Individual Differences Test — Form A

SUBTEST B
16 PF Individual Differences Test — Form C

SUBTEST C
Response to Pictured Situations

On the following pages, you will find 12 sketches of situations in which a person might find himself at some time. In each sketch, one of the persons in the situation has just made a remark. You are asked to supply the response of the second person in the situation as if you were that person. You may make your response as long or as short as you would like. Do not be concerned about staying within the space provided for your answer, or about spelling or cleverness in your answers. Just write down the first reaction which occurs to you in response to the situation depicted. It is your immediate feelings and reactions which we are interested in obtaining.

SUBTEST D
Belief Alternatives

Source: Rotter, J. B. Generalized expectancies for internal versus external control of reinforcement. *Psychological Monographs,* 1966, *80,* 609.

SUBTEST E
Personal Opinion Test

Source: Rokeach, M. "Political and religious dogmatism: An alternative to the authoritarian personality". *Psychological Monographs,* 1956, *70,* 425.

SUBTEST F
Characteristic Quality Test

For the last part of this subtest, use the following lists of 60 characteristics to describe the qualities you believe to be generally associated with **A HOSTAGE, A HOSTAGE-TAKER** and **A NEGOTIATOR.** Place a check (✓) mark within the parenthesis for each characteristic which seems to you to best describe each of these three kinds of people. If, for example, you felt that **HOSTAGES** were in general extremely afraid, you would place a check mark next to the number 4 for that characteristic on the first answer form. Be sure to check mark only one number for each of the characteristics and do not omit any of the items. There are separate sheets for each of the three persons headed **HOSTAGES, HOSTAGE-TAKERS** and **NEGOTIATORS.**

HOSTAGES

		NOT AT ALL	MODERATELY	QUITE	EXTREMELY
1	AFRAID	1 ( )	2 ( )	3 ( )	4 ( )
2	AGITATED	1 ( )	2 ( )	3 ( )	4 ( )
3	ANGRY	1 ( )	2 ( )	3 ( )	4 ( )
4	ANXIOUS	1 ( )	2 ( )	3 ( )	4 ( )
5	ATTENTIVE	1 ( )	2 ( )	3 ( )	4 ( )
6	BOASTFUL	1 ( )	2 ( )	3 ( )	4 ( )
7	BRAVE	1 ( )	2 ( )	3 ( )	4 ( )
8	CALM	1 ( )	2 ( )	3 ( )	4 ( )
9	CARELESS	1 ( )	2 ( )	3 ( )	4 ( )
10	COLD	1 ( )	2 ( )	3 ( )	4 ( )
11	CONFUSED	1 ( )	2 ( )	3 ( )	4 ( )
12	COOPERATIVE	1 ( )	2 ( )	3 ( )	4 ( )
13	COWARDLY	1 ( )	2 ( )	3 ( )	4 ( )
14	CRUEL	1 ( )	2 ( )	3 ( )	4 ( )
15	DECEITFUL	1 ( )	2 ( )	3 ( )	4 ( )
16	DEGENERATE	1 ( )	2 ( )	3 ( )	4 ( )
17	DESTRUCTIVE	1 ( )	2 ( )	3 ( )	4 ( )
18	DISAPPROVING	1 ( )	2 ( )	3 ( )	4 ( )
19	DISTRACTED	1 ( )	2 ( )	3 ( )	4 ( )
20	DRUNKEN	1 ( )	2 ( )	3 ( )	4 ( )
21	EDUCATED	1 ( )	2 ( )	3 ( )	4 ( )
22	EXCITABLE	1 ( )	2 ( )	3 ( )	4 ( )
23	FORGETFUL	1 ( )	2 ( )	3 ( )	4 ( )
24	FRIENDLY	1 ( )	2 ( )	3 ( )	4 ( )
25	GRATEFUL	1 ( )	2 ( )	3 ( )	4 ( )
26	HATEFUL	1 ( )	2 ( )	3 ( )	4 ( )
27	HUMBLE	1 ( )	2 ( )	3 ( )	4 ( )
28	INSANE	1 ( )	2 ( )	3 ( )	4 ( )
29	INTELLIGENT	1 ( )	2 ( )	3 ( )	4 ( )
30	IRRESOLUTE	1 ( )	2 ( )	3 ( )	4 ( )
31	LENIENT	1 ( )	2 ( )	3 ( )	4 ( )
32	MASTERFUL	1 ( )	2 ( )	3 ( )	4 ( )
33	MODEST	1 ( )	2 ( )	3 ( )	4 ( )
34	MYSTIFYING	1 ( )	2 ( )	3 ( )	4 ( )
35	OBEDIENT	1 ( )	2 ( )	3 ( )	4 ( )
36	OBSTINATE	1 ( )	2 ( )	3 ( )	4 ( )
37	PAINSTAKING	1 ( )	2 ( )	3 ( )	4 ( )
38	PATERNAL	1 ( )	2 ( )	3 ( )	4 ( )
39	PESSIMISTIC	1 ( )	2 ( )	3 ( )	4 ( )
40	PREPARED	1 ( )	2 ( )	3 ( )	4 ( )
41	RASH	1 ( )	2 ( )	3 ( )	4 ( )
42	REPENTENT	1 ( )	2 ( )	3 ( )	4 ( )
43	RESISTIVE	1 ( )	2 ( )	3 ( )	4 ( )
44	ROUGH	1 ( )	2 ( )	3 ( )	4 ( )
45	SAD	1 ( )	2 ( )	3 ( )	4 ( )
46	SENSITIVE	1 ( )	2 ( )	3 ( )	4 ( )
47	SIMPLE-MINDED	1 ( )	2 ( )	3 ( )	4 ( )

48 SKILLFUL	1 (	)	2 (	)	3 (	)	4 (	)
49 SOPHISTICATED	1 (	)	2 (	)	3 (	)	4 (	)
50 STUPID	1 (	)	2 (	)	3 (	)	4 (	)
51 SUBMISSIVE	1 (	)	2 (	)	3 (	)	4 (	)
52 SUCCESSFUL	1 (	)	2 (	)	3 (	)	4 (	)
53 TALKATIVE	1 (	)	2 (	)	3 (	)	4 (	)
54 TOUGH	1 (	)	2 (	)	3 (	)	4 (	)
55 UNCERTAIN	1 (	)	2 (	)	3 (	)	4 (	)
56 VAIN	1 (	)	2 (	)	3 (	)	4 (	)
57 VIGILANT	1 (	)	2 (	)	3 (	)	4 (	)
58 VIOLENT	1 (	)	2 (	)	3 (	)	4 (	)
59 WEAK	1 (	)	2 (	)	3 (	)	4 (	)
60 WITHDRAWN	1 (	)	2 (	)	3 (	)	4 (	)

HOSTAGE-TAKERS

	NOT AT ALL		MODERATELY		QUITE		EXTREMELY	
1 AFRAID	1 (	)	2 (	)	3 (	)	4 (	)
2 AGITATED	1 (	)	2 (	)	3 (	)	4 (	)
3 ANGRY	1 (	)	2 (	)	3 (	)	4 (	)
4 ANXIOUS	1 (	)	2 (	)	3 (	)	4 (	)
5 ATTENTIVE	1 (	)	2 (	)	3 (	)	4 (	)
6 BOASTFUL	1 (	)	2 (	)	3 (	)	4 (	)
7 BRAVE	1 (	)	2 (	)	3 (	)	4 (	)
8 CALM	1 (	)	2 (	)	3 (	)	4 (	)
9 CARELESS	1 (	)	2 (	)	3 (	)	4 (	)
10 COLD	1 (	)	2 (	)	3 (	)	4 (	)
11 CONFUSED	1 (	)	2 (	)	3 (	)	4 (	)
12 COOPERATIVE	1 (	)	2 (	)	3 (	)	4 (	)
13 COWARDLY	1 (	)	2 (	)	3 (	)	4 (	)
14 CRUEL	1 (	)	2 (	)	3 (	)	4 (	)
15 DECEITFUL	1 (	)	2 (	)	3 (	)	4 (	)
16 DEGENERATE	1 (	)	2 (	)	3 (	)	4 (	)
17 DESTRUCTIVE	1 (	)	2 (	)	3 (	)	4 (	)
18 DISAPPROVING	1 (	)	2 (	)	3 (	)	4 (	)
19 DISTRACTED	1 (	)	2 (	)	3 (	)	4 (	)
20 DRUNKEN	1 (	)	2 (	)	3 (	)	4 (	)
21 EDUCATED	1 (	)	2 (	)	3 (	)	4 (	)
22 EXCITABLE	1 (	)	2 (	)	3 (	)	4 (	)
23 FORGETFUL	1 (	)	2 (	)	3 (	)	4 (	)
24 FRIENDLY	1 (	)	2 (	)	3 (	)	4 (	)
25 GRATEFUL	1 (	)	2 (	)	3 (	)	4 (	)
26 HATEFUL	1 (	)	2 (	)	3 (	)	4 (	)
27 HUMBLE	1 (	)	2 (	)	3 (	)	4 (	)
28 INSANE	1 (	)	2 (	)	3 (	)	4 (	)
29 INTELLIGENT	1 (	)	2 (	)	3 (	)	4 (	)

30 IRRESOLUTE	1 ( )	2 ( )	3 ( )	4 ( )
31 LENIENT	1 ( )	2 ( )	3 ( )	4 ( )
32 MASTERFUL	1 ( )	2 ( )	3 ( )	4 ( )
33 MODEST	1 ( )	2 ( )	3 ( )	4 ( )
34 MYSTIFYING	1 ( )	2 ( )	3 ( )	4 ( )
35 OBEDIENT	1 ( )	2 ( )	3 ( )	4 ( )
36 OBSTINATE	1 ( )	2 ( )	3 ( )	4 ( )
37 PAINSTAKING	1 ( )	2 ( )	3 ( )	4 ( )
38 PATERNAL	1 ( )	2 ( )	3 ( )	4 ( )
39 PESSIMISTIC	1 ( )	2 ( )	3 ( )	4 ( )
40 PREPARED	1 ( )	2 ( )	3 ( )	4 ( )
41 RASH	1 ( )	2 ( )	3 ( )	4 ( )
42 REPENTENT	1 ( )	2 ( )	3 ( )	4 ( )
43 RESISTIVE	1 ( )	2 ( )	3 ( )	4 ( )
44 ROUGH	1 ( )	2 ( )	3 ( )	4 ( )
45 SAD	1 ( )	2 ( )	3 ( )	4 ( )
46 SENSITIVE	1 ( )	2 ( )	3 ( )	4 ( )
47 SIMPLE-MINDED	1 ( )	2 ( )	3 ( )	4 ( )
48 SKILLFUL	1 ( )	2 ( )	3 ( )	4 ( )
49 SOPHISTICATED	1 ( )	2 ( )	3 ( )	4 ( )
50 STUPID	1 ( )	2 ( )	3 ( )	4 ( )
51 SUBMISSIVE	1 ( )	2 ( )	3 ( )	4 ( )
52 SUCCESSFUL	1 ( )	2 ( )	3 ( )	4 ( )
53 TALKATIVE	1 ( )	2 ( )	3 ( )	4 ( )
54 TOUGH	1 ( )	2 ( )	3 ( )	4 ( )
55 UNCERTAIN	1 ( )	2 ( )	3 ( )	4 ( )
56 VAIN	1 ( )	2 ( )	3 ( )	4 ( )
57 VIGILANT	1 ( )	2 ( )	3 ( )	4 ( )
58 VIOLENT	1 ( )	2 ( )	3 ( )	4 ( )
59 WEAK	1 ( )	2 ( )	3 ( )	4 ( )
60 WITHDRAWN	1 ( )	2 ( )	3 ( )	4 ( )

NEGOTIATORS

	NOT AT ALL	MODERATELY	QUITE	EXTREMELY
1 AFRAID	1 ( )	2 ( )	3 ( )	4 ( )
2 AGITATED	1 ( )	2 ( )	3 ( )	4 ( )
3 ANGRY	1 ( )	2 ( )	3 ( )	4 ( )
4 ANXIOUS	1 ( )	2 ( )	3 ( )	4 ( )
5 ATTENTIVE	1 ( )	2 ( )	3 ( )	4 ( )
6 BOASTFUL	1 ( )	2 ( )	3 ( )	4 ( )
7 BRAVE	1 ( )	2 ( )	3 ( )	4 ( )
8 CALM	1 ( )	2 ( )	3 ( )	4 ( )
9 CARELESS	1 ( )	2 ( )	3 ( )	4 ( )
10 COLD	1 ( )	2 ( )	3 ( )	4 ( )

	1		2		3		4	
11 CONFUSED	1 (	)	2 (	)	3 (	)	4 (	)
12 COOPERATIVE	1 (	)	2 (	)	3 (	)	4 (	)
13 COWARDLY	1 (	)	2 (	)	3 (	)	4 (	)
14 CRUEL	1 (	)	2 (	)	3 (	)	4 (	)
15 DECEITFUL	1 (	)	2 (	)	3 (	)	4 (	)
16 DEGENERATE	1 (	)	2 (	)	3 (	)	4 (	)
17 DESTRUCTIVE	1 (	)	2 (	)	3 (	)	4 (	)
18 DISAPPROVING	1 (	)	2 (	)	3 (	)	4 (	)
19 DISTRACTED	1 (	)	2 (	)	3 (	)	4 (	)
20 DRUNKEN	1 (	)	2 (	)	3 (	)	4 (	)
21 EDUCATED	1 (	)	2 (	)	3 (	)	4 (	)
22 EXCITABLE	1 (	)	2 (	)	3 (	)	4 (	)
23 FORGETFUL	1 (	)	2 (	)	3 (	)	4 (	)
24 FRIENDLY	1 (	)	2 (	)	3 (	)	4 (	)
25 GRATEFUL	1 (	)	2 (	)	3 (	)	4 (	)
26 HATEFUL	1 (	)	2 (	)	3 (	)	4 (	)
27 HUMBLE	1 (	)	2 (	)	3 (	)	4 (	)
28 INSANE	1 (	)	2 (	)	3 (	)	4 (	)
29 INTELLIGENT	1 (	)	2 (	)	3 (	)	4 (	)
30 IRRESOLUTE	1 (	)	2 (	)	3 (	)	4 (	)
31 LENIENT	1 (	)	2 (	)	3 (	)	4 (	)
32 MASTERFUL	1 (	)	2 (	)	3 (	)	4 (	)
33 MODEST	1 (	)	2 (	)	3 (	)	4 (	)
34 MYSTIFYING	1 (	)	2 (	)	3 (	)	4 (	)
35 OBEDIENT	1 (	)	2 (	)	3 (	)	4 (	)
36 OBSTINATE	1 (	)	2 (	)	3 (	)	4 (	)
37 PAINSTAKING	1 (	)	2 (	)	3 (	)	4 (	)
38 PATERNAL	1 (	)	2 (	)	3 (	)	4 (	)
39 PESSIMISTIC	1 (	)	2 (	)	3 (	)	4 (	)
40 PREPARED	1 (	)	2 (	)	3 (	)	4 (	)
41 RASH	1 (	)	2 (	)	3 (	)	4 (	)
42 REPENTENT	1 (	)	2 (	)	3 (	)	4 (	)
43 RESISTIVE	1 (	)	2 (	)	3 (	)	4 (	)
44 ROUGH	1 (	)	2 (	)	3 (	)	4 (	)
45 SAD	1 (	)	2 (	)	3 (	)	4 (	)
46 SENSITIVE	1 (	)	2 (	)	3 (	)	4 (	)
47 SIMPLE-MINDED	1 (	)	2 (	)	3 (	)	4 (	)
48 SKILLFUL	1 (	)	2 (	)	3 (	)	4 (	)
49 SOPHISTICATED	1 (	)	2 (	)	3 (	)	4 (	)
50 STUPID	1 (	)	2 (	)	3 (	)	4 (	)
51 SUBMISSIVE	1 (	)	2 (	)	3 (	)	4 (	)
52 SUCCESSFUL	1 (	)	2 (	)	3 (	)	4 (	)
53 TALKATIVE	1 (	)	2 (	)	3 (	)	4 (	)
54 TOUGH	1 (	)	2 (	)	3 (	)	4 (	)
55 UNCERTAIN	1 (	)	2 (	)	3 (	)	4 (	)
56 VAIN	1 (	)	2 (	)	3 (	)	4 (	)
57 VIGILANT	1 (	)	2 (	)	3 (	)	4 (	)
58 VIOLENT	1 (	)	2 (	)	3 (	)	4 (	)
59 WEAK	1 (	)	2 (	)	3 (	)	4 (	)
60 WITHDRAWN	1 (	)	2 (	)	3 (	)	4 (	)

Appendix B
Recommended Readings

I. Hostage/Terrorism
1. Bassiouni, M.E. (Ed.). *International terrorism and political crimes.* Springfield, IL: Charles C. Thomas, 1975.
2. Bell, J. B. *Transnational terror.* Washington, DC: American Enterprise Institute for Public Policy Research, 1975.
3. Burton, A. *Urban terrorism.* New York: Free Press, 1975.
4. Clutterbuck, R. *Living with terrorism.* New Rochelle, NY: Arlington House, 1975.
5. Hacker, F. J. *Crusaders, criminals, crazies.* New York: W. W. Norton, 1976.
6. Momboisse, R. M. *Riots, revolts and insurrections.* Springfield, IL: Charles C. Thomas, 1967.
7. Parry, A. *Terrorism, from Robespierre to Arafat.* New York: Vanguard Press, 1976.

II. Police Tactics
8. Armstrong, T. R., & Cinnamon, K. M. *Power and authority in law enforcement.* Springfield, IL: Charles C. Thomas, 1976.
9. Brooks, P. R. *Officer down, code three.* Schiller Park, IL: Motorola Teleprograms, 1975.

10. Goldstein, A. P., Monti, P. J., Sardino, T. J., & Green, D. J. *Police crisis intervention.* Kalamazoo: Behaviordelia, 1976.
11. Hoobler, R. L. *Police tactics in hazardous situations.* St. Paul: West Publishing Co., 1976.
12. Kroes, W. H., & Hurrell, J. J. *Job stress and the police officer.* Washington, DC: National Institute for Occupational Safety and Health, 1976.
13. Vandall, F. J. *Police training for tough calls.* Atlanta: Emory University, 1976.

III. Negotiation
14. Baer, W. E. *Grievance handling.* New York: American Management Association, 1970.
15. Cohen, A. R. *Attitude change and social influence.* New York: Random House, 1966.
16. Karlins, M., & Abelson, H. I. *Persuasion.* New York: Springer, 1970.
17. Nierenberg, G. I. *The art of negotiating.* New York: Cornerstone Library, 1968.
18. Rubin, J. Z., & Brown, B. R. *The social psychology of bargaining and negotiation.* New York: Academic Press, 1975.
19. Schrank, J. *Deception detection.* Boston: Beacon Press, 1975.
20. Towers, B., Whittingham, T. G., & Gottschalk, A. W. *Bargaining for change.* London: George Allen, 1972.

IV. Abnormal Behavior
21. Davison, G. C., & Neale, J. M. *Abnormal psychology.* New York: Wiley, 1974.
22. Green, E. J. *Psychology for law enforcement.* New York: Wiley, 1976.
23. Parker, L. C., & Meier, R. D. *Interpersonal psychology for law enforcement and corrections.* St. Paul: West Publishing Co., 1975.
24. Reiser, M. *Practical psychology for police officers.* Springfield, IL: Charles C. Thomas, 1973.
25. Russell, H. E., & Beigel, A. *Understanding human behavior for effective police work.* New York: Basic Books, 1976.
26. Schlossberg, H. *Psychologist with a gun.* New York: Coward, McCann & Geoghegan, 1974.

27. Steinberg, J. L., & McEvoy, D. W. *The police and the behavioral sciences.* Springfield, IL: Charles C. Thomas, 1974.
28. Watson, N.A. *Issues in human relations.* Gaithersburg, MD: International Association of Chiefs of Police, 1973.

V. Aggression
29. Goldstein, J. H. *Aggression and crimes of violence.* New York: Oxford University Press, 1975.
30. Johnson, R. N. *Aggression in man and animals.* Philadelphia: W. B. Saunders, 1972.
31. Toch, H. *Police, prisons and the problems of violence.* Washington, DC: National Institute of Mental Health, 1977.
32. Toplin, R. B. *Unchallenged violence.* Westport, CT: Greenwood Press, 1975.
33. Westley, W. A. *Violence and the police.* Cambridge, MA: MIT Press, 1970.

VI. Aggression Management
34. Filley, A. E. *Interpersonal conflict resolution.* Glenview, IL: Scott, Foresman & Co., 1974.
35. Knutson, J. F. (Ed.). *The control of aggression.* Chicago: Aldine, 1973.
36. Schonborn, K. *Dealing with violence.* Springfield, IL: Charles C. Thomas, 1975.
37. Singer, J. L. (Ed.). *The control of aggression and violence.* New York: Academic Press, 1971.
38. Smith, C. G., (Ed.). *Conflict resolution: Contributions of the behavioral sciences.* South Bend, IN: University of Notre Dame Press, 1971.

VII. The Media
39. Bremen, P. Television's dilemma: Stay on the air—or bail out? The Quill, 1977, 65, p. 8.
40. Crisis cop raps media.*More,* June, 1977, pp. 18-21.
41. Czerniejewshi, H. J. Guidelines for the coverage of terrorism. *The Quill,* 1977, 65, pp. 21-23.
42. Denton, T. Fair to be middlin? The newsman as negotiator. *The Quill,* 1974, 62, pp. 13-17.
43. Fenyvesi, C. Looking into the muzzle of terrorists. *The Quill,* 1977, 65, pp. 16-18.

44. Howitt, D., & Cumberbatch, G. *Mass media violence and society.* New York: Wiley, 1975.
45. Johnson, N. Television and violence. *Television Quarterly,* 1969, 8, 30-69.

VIII. Police Training

46. Auten, J. H. *Training in the small department.* Springfield, IL: Charles C. Thomas, 1973.
47. Goldstein, A.P. *Structured learning therapy.* New York: Academic Press, 1973.
48. Joyce, B., & Weil, M. *Models of teaching.* Englewood Cliffs, NJ: Prentice-Hall, 1972.
49. Klotter, J. C. *Techniques for police instructors.* Springfield, IL: Charles C. Thomas, 1963.

Notes

Notes